Library Alive!

Promoting reading and research
in the school library

Gwen Gawith

A & C Black · London

Gawith, Gwen
    Library Alive!
1. School children—Great Britain—Library orientation
I. Title
025.5   Z711.2

ISBN 0-7136-2900-2

A&C Black (Publishers) Limited,
35 Bedford Row, London WC1R 4JH

This edition © 1987 A&C Black (Publishers) Limited
Reprinted 1988

First published 1983 Longman Paul Limited, New Zealand,
with the title Library Alive! © 1983 Longman Paul Limited

ISBN 0-7136-2900-2

Acknowledgement
The cover illustration is by Sarah Pooley

Contents

Introduction

When *Library Alive!* first came into our hands we showed it to the teacher librarians who were attending our in-service course in School Library Studies. Enthusiasm is a mild word to describe their reaction; whether from primary, secondary or special schools they wanted to rush off and use the ideas and the materials with their pupils and their colleagues. We are delighted that *Library Alive!* is now available in this country and pleased to be asked to write this new introduction. We do so confident that other teachers will find it as helpful and practical as have those who queued up to borrow it from us.

School Libraries: The Foundation of the Curriculum is the title of the report of the LISC (Libraries and Information Services Council) working party, published in 1984. This choice of title is significant, requiring us to question current attitudes and practice. How many schools see the library in this central role? The report looks at the school library, not only in terms of levels of provision of books, materials, staff and space but, more essentially, in terms of the learning needs of children. It argues that the library has a central role in the school curriculum and that the development of library and information skills are at its foundation. Only when all teachers are involved in tasks that introduce and consolidate these skills as part of normal classroom learning across the curriculum will the need for libraries and their resources be clear, and children given the opportunities and facilities they deserve. The report urges all schools to develop a policy for information skills across the curriculum; in this process the library comes alive as an integral part of learning and teaching.

In primary, secondary and special schools, the teacher librarian needs to give a lead to colleagues in formulating activities and familiarising both staff and pupils with search and find procedures. Some of these will be taught in the library but this should not mean just a programme of 'Library lessons' taught in isolation from the rest of the curriculum. Particularly in secondary schools, 'Library' frequently appears almost as a subject on the timetable. (Often the only time when pupils have the opportunity or need to be there.) Library lessons or Library time, in many cases the result of hard-fought battles by librarians or conscientiously donated by the English department, although well intentioned have not in the main produced the kind of active independent problem-solvers and discriminating readers who will be able to cope with the demands of a rapidly changing world. Some years ago, the Bullock report (*A Language for Life*) commented: 'All too often pupils are taught how to locate and handle books but not given the immediate opportunity to put (these skills) to a useful purpose as opposed to an artificially contrived one.' That statement remains largely true today. The same report urged schools to increase the range and amount of children's voluntary reading. Successive surveys point to the competing attractions of television, video, computers and popular music and show that it is not enough simply to make books available. Happily they also show that, in a context where a positive attitude to books is created and where informed advice is available, children do become readers.

How can *Library Alive!* help in this situation?

- It offers a well thought out and lively approach to the development of information skills and the encouragement of reading for pleasure.

- It gives immediate assistance to the teacher librarian or enthusiastic teacher who is trying to lead discussion about these issues. The examples in the book provide a focus for discussion and a sense of what might be achieved.

- The activities suggested here can be undertaken by any teacher who lacks the time or perhaps the expertise to design and produce his or her own learning materials. They are offered copyright free for reproduction and can be used as they stand or modified to meet the needs of particular children.

- The activities are presented in a numbered sequence but are designed for selective use, not to be worked through from beginning to end. They provide an introduction to and practice in skills, and can be used either in lessons in the library or in contextual teaching which arises naturally out of the concerns of the classroom. They serve a two-fold purpose: they isolate a particular skill or focus and give out-of-context practice so that the pupil can then apply it in the learning context given the opportunity and encouragement to do so; they also allow the teacher to monitor each pupil's attitude and ability to apply the skills, providing a useful diagnostic tool. The skills index which refers to numbered activities will help teacher librarians and teachers to introduce or reinforce particular skills in a variety of learning contexts.

The activities offered in *Library Alive!* are also FUN – a much neglected aspect of learning, especially in learning about libraries.

The LISC report and others show that in too many schools, the library is the place which pupils visit only to get out of the cold, or to avoid being bullied; the place where they are sent to change their unread book or to 'look things up' without any real idea how to go about it. The knowledge that there is good practice in some schools, that we can find groups of children who read avidly, track down information like bloodhounds and are clearly at home with libraries, that some schools have full-time qualified librarians, or trained teacher librarians, and/or good support from the School Library Service only intensifies the darkness elsewhere. In many schools, we find enthusiastic teachers with responsibility for the library feeling isolated and unsupported.

Changing this requires a change of attitude in schools. The quality of learning in a school will depend on the extent to which all those in it stop regarding the library merely as a room for storing books, and instead promote it as the centre for learning and enjoyment. Children should know how to use the library and its systems, but more importantly, they should *want* to use the library. Why bother to pit your wits against a bewildering maze of numbers and letters when books are 'a load of rubbish' anyway? Learning to use the catalogue, the subject index and even the Dewey Decimal classification system must become the gateway to a world a child wants to enter.

The teacher and teacher librarian should be the 'open sesame' to enjoyment of the library, not uninterested by-standers or key-jangling custodians of a storehouse. Bringing the library alive for its users involves more than the traditional promotional activities: display posters, book weeks and visiting authors organised by one enthusiast. It is an attitude of mind which underlies the way in which every teacher presents library and learning to the pupils. It is an attitude of mind that GCSE has made urgently necessary and one which already has a firm place in the best primary practice, from the early years.

To effect this change requires an agreed approach throughout a school. There can be no one definite way of managing this. Like booklists, approaches are best tailored to reflect the resources, needs and attitudes of individual teachers and schools. However, moving forward can often be helped by having a framework to focus discussion, to encourage the best use of the school's resources and give the efforts of individual teachers cohesion and continuity.

The subsequent pages offer a framework for promoting the library.

Jenny Parmenter, Principal Lecturer, Library Department
Pat Triggs, Senior Lecturer, Department of Education
Co-tutors for the DIPSE in School Library Studies, Bristol Polytechnic.

A Framework for Promotion

Who

Promotion is easier to plan with specific people and their needs in mind.

A library service is more effective if it is based on a survey which establishes who the users are and what they see as their reading and information needs. Finding out stated and potential needs and interests is particularly important in a school library where the child may not be a member of a public library and needs to be helped to establish an identity as a library user and borrower. Children who are made to feel like 'real' borrowers with a vested interest in the library, its stock, systems and routines, will become regular library users. This is different from feeling like one of a class of thirty shunted in for weekly book changing.

A positive approach is essential whether in primary, secondary or special school. Becoming familiar with the library can be greatly helped by activities, good visual signposting within the library and a conscious effort by all teachers to develop and reinforce attitudes and skills through enjoyable classroom and library work.

Let pupils know that their reading interests and enthusiasms will affect book purchase and library activities. For instance, if there seems to be an enormous interest in motocross and your school library can afford only one or two additions, you should be able to obtain a supplementary loan from the School Library Service, or invite the local public librarian to bring some books to share and perhaps ask the local bookseller or the school bookshop supplier to provide titles for a special display. You might even be able to invite a local motocross rider to bring a bike to school and give a talk. The important thing is that such activities arise out of users' expressed needs and interests.

What

Once you have defined the users and have a clear idea of their wants and needs, the next step is to look closely at what you are going to promote.

Promotion of the library service has many different facets and, although these are interdependent, it is useful to look at them separately.

1. Promotion of the library itself, meaning the promotion of all learning resources within the school. 'Library' in a school should mean more than the room which carries the label. No matter where resources are stored, they need to be organised and made available by means of a unified system which works for the benefit of all users, according to their needs.

2. Promotion of the books and materials stored in the central, classroom or departmental collections.

3. Promotion of the library's systems designed to record and encourage systematic retrieval of stored information.

4. Promotion of reading and enjoyment of resources – fiction, non-fiction, book, non-book.

Where

The library itself should encourage people to use and enjoy it.

A bright uncluttered well-signposted, attractive library with comfortable seating, lots of face-out books, displays, plants, community information, and tidy shelves with bright, neatly processed books will get the use it deserves. Dark, dank places equipped with tattered, fading, out-of-date books, piles of dusty materials waiting for attention, no colour, 'Do Not' notices, no signposting or guidance will get an appropriate response. It's less a question of money than an attitude of mind.

Environment

Carefully planned layout and design will encourage children to be independent users and retrievers of information in all forms.

Try to provide:
An informal reading area where pupils can relax on cushions, bean bags or low chairs with low tables and not too much immediate activity around them.

A work area with tables, chairs and good lighting, close to the non-fiction and reference sections and catalogue, if possible in a quiet place.

Clear guidance to use of the library, use of the catalogue, subject index and specialised sections and resources. Professional, eye-catching notices set the tone.

A layout which encourages easy and logical use.

Colour, texture and points of visual interest such as plants, display/notice boards for school, community and current events.

Variety in display techniques and promotion.

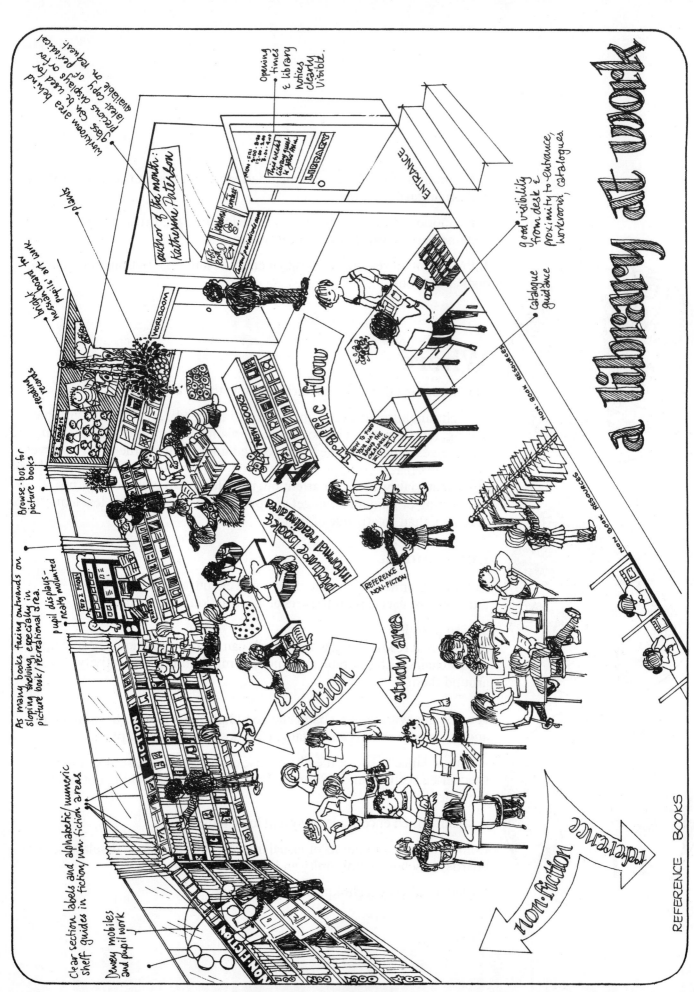

a library at work

REFERENCE BOOKS

Stock

Each book should be able to defend its place on the library shelf in terms of physical condition, date of publication, appropriateness of reading and interest level and factual accuracy and relevance. Tidy, well-guided shelves displaying as much of the stock face-out as space permits, with attractive well-maintained and spine-labelled books all help to promote interest.

Displays

Displays often occupy a disproportionate amount of the teacher librarian's time. They are only one form of visual promotion and not the whole task. Display is always more effective if it reflects the interests and needs of the pupils, or if the pupils have contributed towards it in some way. It is more effective still if there is carry-over into curriculum-related work, or if it is a library extension of classroom work. The most important message, that old displays are dead displays, applies, and displays should be planned with this in mind.

When

Learning how to find information from books and libraries should not be regarded as something additional to or apart from classroom work. Nor is it something to be started at the top of the junior school or in the early secondary years. Becoming a confident library user starts with a child's first encounters with books. An introduction to an organised library can begin in the infant school. The successful school library is one that is integral to the teachers' teaching and the pupils' learning. Reading and guided research using the library should be part of learning. Once again the prerequisite seems to be an attitude of mind rather than a definable amount of time.

Book weeks, book fairs and other promotional activities focus the school's attention on books and reading for a limited period and give promotion an effective short-term focus. However, only a year-long sustained effort can produce confident, independent library and information users.

Some suggestions for making the library central to learning. All teachers can:

1. Help the children to think of themselves as library users and readers, encourage them to keep library folders or some form of reading records and talk to children about these at regular intervals. Make suggestions for further interesting reading and share experiences and responses.

2. Help children to become familiar with library layout and systems by giving practice in the requisite skills and encouraging pupils to apply them in their classroom work and research.

3. Encourage children to value books and evaluate the printed word, reading daily from novels, non-fiction, poetry, riddles, jokes, biographies, newspaper articles and magazines.

4. Help children of all ages to enjoy and value illustration by looking at picture books and illustrated texts regularly.

5. Encourage children to get to know different authors, by introducing their books, providing listening or 'taster' tapes, researching their backgrounds, encouraging pupils to write to them and arranging visits if possible.

6. Help children to understand how a book is made and encourage the children to participate in 'the publishing process'.

7. Provide a regular block of time each day for independent reading of material of the pupil's own choice. Many primary schools set aside a time when the whole school stops to read, including the head and staff.

8. Encourage pupils to contribute to individual and class displays, join reviewing groups, compile booklists and data banks and read aloud to younger children.

9. Give status and value to book-related work by displaying it effectively.

10. Use the library's resources imaginatively, to show that you see it as much more than just a place for storing materials.

11. Provide a structured training programme for children who want to be library monitors or librarians.

12. Encourage teachers and pupils to take turns in being responsible for a library display.

13. Use assembly to tell pupils and teachers about new developments or acquisitions and to encourage them to share the results of their enquiries and reading.

14. Organise special activities – a competition, a special library guest, a Book Day, a sponsored read-in.

Although, finally, the responsibility for much of this promotion will rest on the teacher librarian, or member of staff responsible for the library, the impact in the school will depend on everyone's commitment and effort.

For any teacher, the development and implementation of a library programme single-handed is a suicidal prospect in the light of time available. For each teacher to co-operate with and contribute to a total school effort is not unrealistic. In many of the activities above, the teachers' role is to encourage pupils to participate as fully as possible in the running and promotion of their own library. The answer to the 'When?' question is a shared commitment by staff and pupils to promote the best use of the library and its resources as an integral part of the curriculum.

How

Although promotion of the library and resources must be a co-operative effort, the role of the teacher librarian is very important. Whether a school is successful in establishing a lively library as a focus for its curriculum depends very much on this person. As well as being responsible for the day to day running of the library, the teacher librarian needs to take the lead in establishing the contacts which will make promoting the library a realistic and achievable undertaking.

Liaison with colleagues

This can help to make a bridge between the library and teachers who may be isolated in curriculum areas or classroom units, by concentrating the attention of all teachers on the resources available for learning and on how they can best be used and improved. The teacher librarian also needs to gain the co-operation of all teachers in establishing and carrying out an agreed approach to developing library and information skills.

Liaison with other agencies

The teacher librarian is part of a wider professional network. Links should be made with the School Library Service, the Public Library Service, the Museum Service, the world of publishing and bookselling. In this way the teacher librarian gains support and practical help from like-minded colleagues with special expertise and the school's library and its users find themselves part of a wider context of books and learning materials.

The Library Committee

Establishing a Library Committee which operates as a policy making and consultative group for the school can be influential in ensuring the success of library promotion. Such a group, operating at the highest level, can be useful in establishing a school approach to selection policy, setting priorities, agreeing procedures, facilitating liaison and supporting library initiatives. It can also be a useful forum for seeking parental involvement and opinion.

Library Users' Committees

Setting up User Groups can be an effective way of involving pupils, staff and parents to review and improve the organisation and running of the library. They can be a useful focus for planning special events and for co-ordinating volunteer help.

Voluntary help

Most school libraries rely very heavily on volunteer help of all kinds to ensure their smooth running and, in some cases, to improve the quality of provision and service.

Involving parents as makers of equipment, clerical support, library assistants, storytellers, book sharers and book event helpers is one way of establishing valuable links between home and school.

The degree of pupils' involvement in the running and promotion of the library is directly related to the success of the library as an integral part of their learning. Library monitors should be given the appropriate library training and be fully involved in library matters. As well as routine duties, they should be given additional responsibilities and the status that earns – helping to organise displays, run the bookshop and secondhand book swaps, playing host to special visitors and researching the book and information needs of other pupils.

The 'How?' of library promotion is dependent on a library policy agreed by the whole school, co-ordinated by the teacher librarian and implemented by a blend of staff, pupils and parents. All putting into practice exactly the right mix of **who, what, where,** and **when.**

PROMOTION ACTIVITIES

1

READER PROFILE

9 years and up

ANSWER THE QUESTIONS
AND STICK THE COMPLETED
READER PROFILE INTO YOUR
LIBRARY FOLDER OR LIBRARY
LOG. (see page 14)

What I'd like someone to write is a story about a guy called SuperSam who trains his dog, Superbark, to follow a smell like police dogs can. One day some new sports equipment is stolen from SuperSam's school. SuperSam was out of the classroom at the time. Can Superbark prove he is not guilty?

READER PROFILE

NAME .... CLASS .... AGE ....

DO YOU FIND READING   EASY ☐   FUN ☐   HARD WORK ☐   BORING ☐

CAN YOU FIND THE SORT OF BOOKS YOU LIKE IN THE LIBRARY?   YES ☐   NO ☐

LIST SOME OF THE BOOKS YOU HAVE ENJOYED:

_____

_____

NAME YOUR FAVOURITE AUTHORS:

_____

_____

BORROWER'S FINGERPRINT

WHAT ARE YOUR HOBBIES AND INTERESTS?

_____

_____

WHICH SPORTS ARE YOU INTERESTED IN? _____

_____

WHAT IS YOUR FAVOURITE TV PROGRAMME? _____

WHY? _____

IF YOU COULD HAVE A BOOK WRITTEN SPECIALLY FOR YOU, WHAT WOULD IT BE ABOUT? WOULD IT BE AN ADVENTURE, OR A MYSTERY, OR A FAMILY STORY, OR A SCHOOL STORY? WOULD IT BE HAPPY OR SAD, OR SAD WITH A HAPPY ENDING, OR WOULD IT BE EXCITING OR FUNNY? WOULD IT BE ABOUT PEOPLE OR ANIMALS? WOULD IT BE ABOUT THE REAL WORLD, OR A WORLD OF MAKE-BELIEVE?

WRITE ABOUT IT, GIVE IT A TITLE AND DRAW A PICTURE OF THE COVER

_____

TITLE

SUPERSAM OF THE 1980's

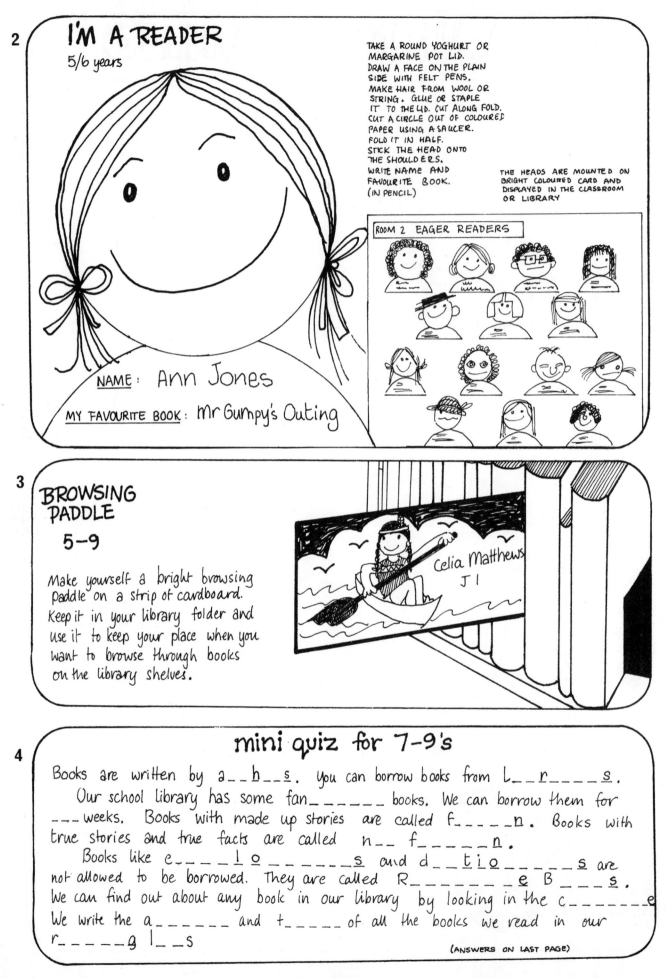

2

I'M A READER
5/6 years

NAME: Ann Jones

MY FAVOURITE BOOK: Mr Gumpy's Outing

TAKE A ROUND YOGHURT OR
MARGARINE POT LID.
DRAW A FACE ON THE PLAIN
SIDE WITH FELT PENS.
MAKE HAIR FROM WOOL OR
STRING. GLUE OR STAPLE
IT TO THE LID. CUT ALONG FOLD.
CUT A CIRCLE OUT OF COLOURED
PAPER USING A SAUCER.
FOLD IT IN HALF.
STICK THE HEAD ONTO
THE SHOULDERS.
WRITE NAME AND
FAVOURITE BOOK.
(IN PENCIL)

THE HEADS ARE MOUNTED ON
BRIGHT COLOURED CARD AND
DISPLAYED IN THE CLASSROOM
OR LIBRARY

ROOM 2 EAGER READERS

3

BROWSING PADDLE
5-9

Make yourself a bright browsing
paddle on a strip of cardboard.
Keep it in your library folder and
use it to keep your place when you
want to browse through books
on the library shelves.

Celia Matthews
J 1

4

mini quiz for 7-9's

Books are written by a__h__s. You can borrow books from L__r_____s.
    Our school library has some fan_____ books. We can borrow them for
___ weeks. Books with made up stories are called f_____n. Books with
true stories and true facts are called n__ f_____n.
    Books like e____l_o_____s and d__tio_____s are
not allowed to be borrowed. They are called R_____ e B___s.
We can find out about any book in our library by looking in the c_____e
We write the a_____ and t_____ of all the books we read in our
r_____g l__s

(ANSWERS ON LAST PAGE)

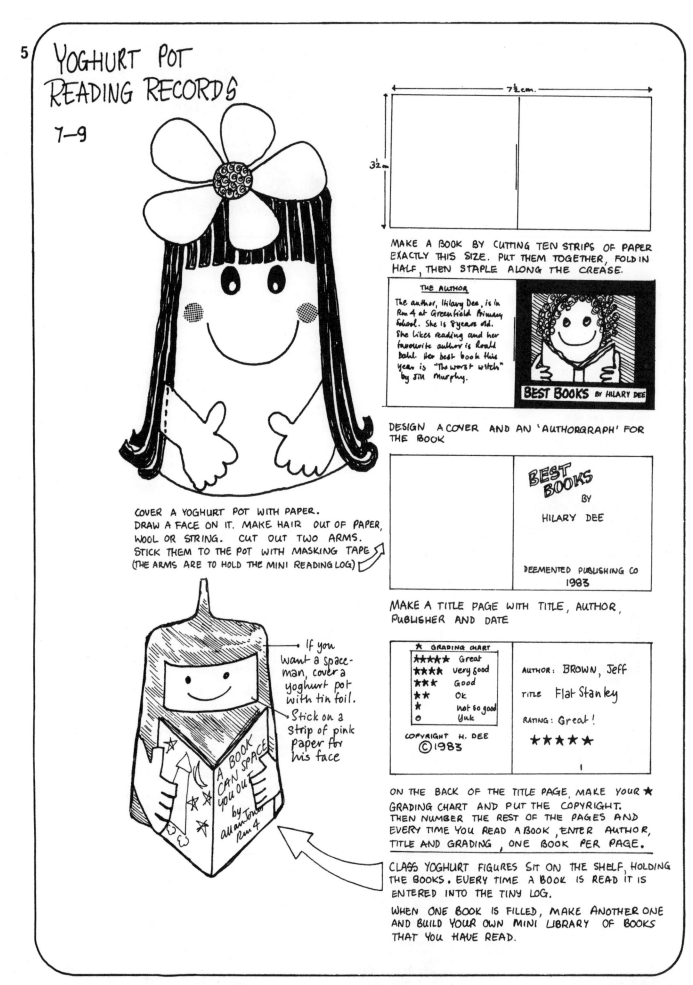

5 YOGHURT POT READING RECORDS

7-9

7½ cm.

3½ cm

MAKE A BOOK BY CUTTING TEN STRIPS OF PAPER EXACTLY THIS SIZE. PUT THEM TOGETHER, FOLD IN HALF, THEN STAPLE ALONG THE CREASE.

THE AUTHOR

The author, Hilary Dee, is in Rm 4 at Greenfield Primary School. She is 9 years old. She likes reading and her favourite author is Roald Dahl. Her best book this year is "The worst witch" by Jill Murphy.

BEST BOOKS BY HILARY DEE

DESIGN A COVER AND AN 'AUTHORGRAPH' FOR THE BOOK

COVER A YOGHURT POT WITH PAPER. DRAW A FACE ON IT. MAKE HAIR OUT OF PAPER, WOOL OR STRING. CUT OUT TWO ARMS. STICK THEM TO THE POT WITH MASKING TAPE (THE ARMS ARE TO HOLD THE MINI READING LOG)

BEST BOOKS BY HILARY DEE

DEEMENTED PUBLISHING CO 1983

MAKE A TITLE PAGE WITH TITLE, AUTHOR, PUBLISHER AND DATE

- If you want a spaceman, cover a yoghurt pot with tin foil.
- Stick on a strip of pink paper for his face

A BOOK CAN SPACE YOU OUT by Allan Jones, Rm 4

★ GRADING CHART	
★★★★★	Great
★★★★	Very good
★★★	Good
★★	Ok
★	Not so good
○	Yuk

COPYRIGHT H. DEE © 1983

AUTHOR: BROWN, Jeff

TITLE Flat Stanley

RATING: Great!

★★★★★

1

ON THE BACK OF THE TITLE PAGE, MAKE YOUR ★ GRADING CHART AND PUT THE COPYRIGHT. THEN NUMBER THE REST OF THE PAGES AND EVERY TIME YOU READ A BOOK, ENTER AUTHOR, TITLE AND GRADING, ONE BOOK PER PAGE.

CLASS YOGHURT FIGURES SIT ON THE SHELF, HOLDING THE BOOKS. EVERY TIME A BOOK IS READ IT IS ENTERED INTO THE TINY LOG.

WHEN ONE BOOK IS FILLED, MAKE ANOTHER ONE AND BUILD YOUR OWN MINI LIBRARY OF BOOKS THAT YOU HAVE READ.

6

LIBRARY FOLDER

9yrs and up

TAKE AN OLD RECORD JACKET (ASK A RECORD SHOP FOR OLD PUBLICITY COVERS) OR MAKE YOUR OWN FOLDER.
THINK UP AN EYE-CATCHING SLOGAN TO PROMOTE READING AND LIBRARIES. PUT THIS SLOGAN AND YOUR NAME AND CLASS ON THE FOLDER.
FOLDERS ARE KEPT IN CLASS SETS AND INTO THEM GO LIBRARY HANDOUTS, EXERCISES AND LOGS FOR THE YEAR.

7

LIBRARY LOG

9yrs and up

TAKE AN EXERCISE BOOK AND MAKE:
1. A <u>DUSTJACKET</u> WITH A <u>BLURB</u>
2. THE <u>TITLE PAGE</u> WITH <u>COPYRIGHT</u>
3. <u>CONTENTS PAGE</u>
4. <u>INTRODUCTION</u> AND <u>LIBRARY MAP</u>
5. <u>READER'S PROFILE</u>

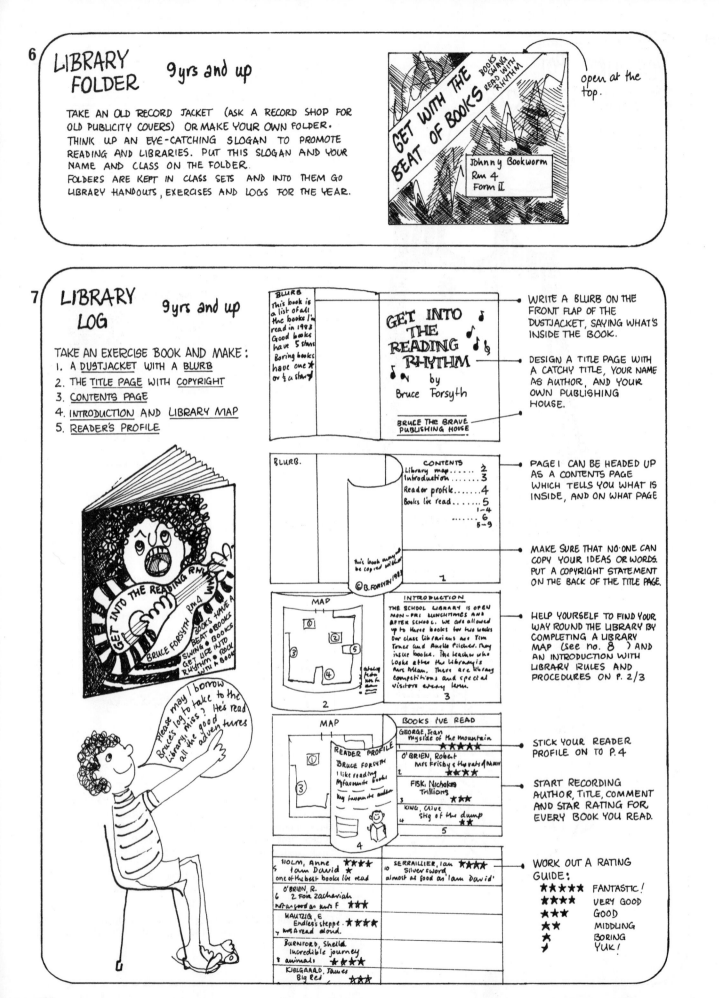

WRITE A BLURB ON THE FRONT FLAP OF THE DUSTJACKET, SAYING WHAT'S INSIDE THE BOOK.

DESIGN A TITLE PAGE WITH A CATCHY TITLE, YOUR NAME AS AUTHOR, AND YOUR OWN PUBLISHING HOUSE.

PAGE 1 CAN BE HEADED UP AS A CONTENTS PAGE WHICH TELLS YOU WHAT IS INSIDE, AND ON WHAT PAGE

MAKE SURE THAT NO-ONE CAN COPY YOUR IDEAS OR WORDS. PUT A COPYRIGHT STATEMENT ON THE BACK OF THE TITLE PAGE.

HELP YOURSELF TO FIND YOUR WAY ROUND THE LIBRARY BY COMPLETING A LIBRARY MAP (see no. 8) AND AN INTRODUCTION WITH LIBRARY RULES AND PROCEDURES ON P. 2/3

STICK YOUR READER PROFILE ON TO P.4

START RECORDING AUTHOR, TITLE, COMMENT AND STAR RATING FOR EVERY BOOK YOU READ.

WORK OUT A RATING GUIDE:

★★★★★ FANTASTIC!
★★★★ VERY GOOD
★★★ GOOD
★★ MIDDLING
★ BORING
⯪ YUK!

8 LIBRARY MAP
9 and up

Ⓐ ENTRANCE
Ⓑ ISSUE DESK
Ⓒ RETURNS BIN FOR RETURNED BOOKS
Ⓓ NON FICTION SHEWES
Ⓔ FICTION SHELVES
Ⓕ REFERENCE BOOKS
Ⓖ CATALOGUE
Ⓗ SUBJECT INDEX
Ⓘ PERIODICALS / MAGAZINES
Ⓙ VERTICAL FILE
Ⓚ BOOK DISPLAYS
Ⓛ LIBRARY NOTICES

DRAW A MAP OF YOUR LIBRARY WITH SHELVES ETC. AND SHOW Ⓐ — Ⓛ ON IT.

Library Map

(Better still, ask your teacher to supply a ready-drawn map to each pupil. You complete the map and keep it safely in your library folder, or stick it into your library log.)

9

BOOK CARE BOOK MARKS OR POSTERS   ALL AGES

AFTER YOU HAVE DISCUSSED BOOK CARE WITH YOUR TEACHER, MAKE A BOOKMARK OR POSTER LIKE THE ONES SHOWN BELOW.

● YOUR TEACHER COULD PHOTOCOPY THE BEST BOOKMARKS AND YOU COULD SELL THEM AT THE SCHOOL FAIR TO RAISE MONEY FOR NEW BOOKS.

● BOOKMARKS CAN ALSO BE MADE INTO MOBILES TO DECORATE YOUR LIBRARY OR CLASSROOM

● KEEP YOUR BEST BOOKMARK TO USE IN THE BOOKS YOU READ.

THIS IS TO CERTIFY THAT John Thomas IS A MEMBER OF THE S.P.C.B. AND WILL HEREAFTER ACT TO PREVENT CRUELTY TO BOOKS CAUSED BY CARELESS HANDLING AND CARRYING

signed 10/2/1983
Jim Brown
Teacher-librarian
SPCB: SOCIETY FOR THE PREVENTION OF CRUELTY TO BOOKS

CLEAN HANDS CLEAN BOOKS

I am your friend
BOOKS ARE FRIENDS
Friends don't like to be
• Thumped and bumped
• Torn and scribbled on
• Wiped with greasy fingers
• Spattered with food and drink
• Bent backwards

PLEASE TREAT ME LIKE A FRIEND – WITH CARE AND COURTESY AND LOVE

YOU CAN'T KISS A TORN BOOK BETTER WITH A BAND AID !

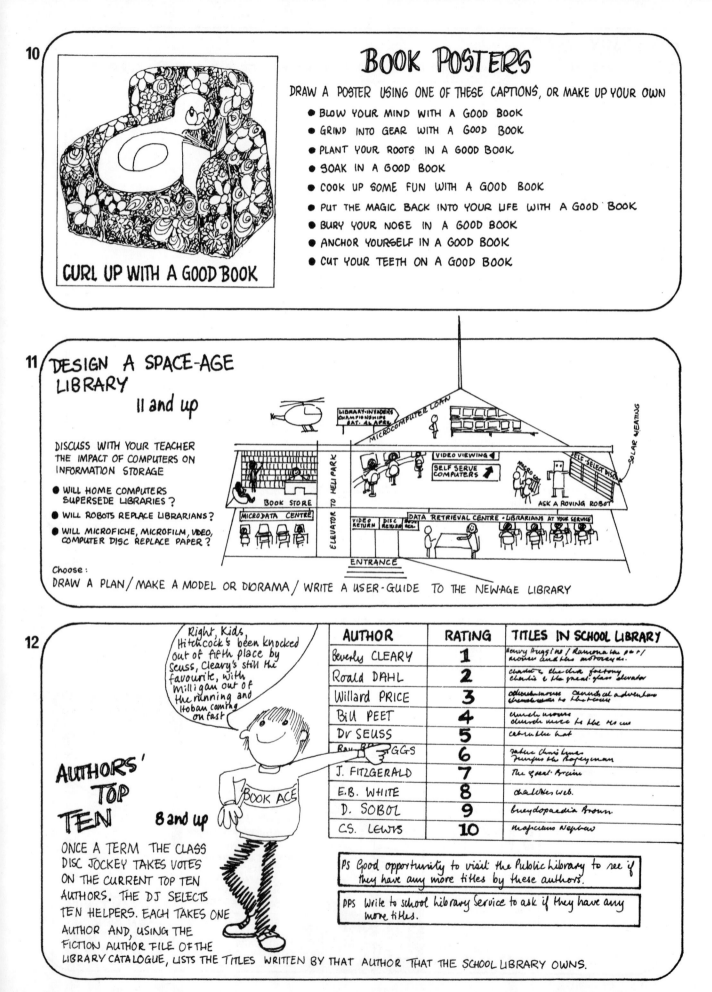

10

BOOK POSTERS

DRAW A POSTER USING ONE OF THESE CAPTIONS, OR MAKE UP YOUR OWN

- BLOW YOUR MIND WITH A GOOD BOOK
- GRIND INTO GEAR WITH A GOOD BOOK
- PLANT YOUR ROOTS IN A GOOD BOOK
- SOAK IN A GOOD BOOK
- COOK UP SOME FUN WITH A GOOD BOOK
- PUT THE MAGIC BACK INTO YOUR LIFE WITH A GOOD BOOK
- BURY YOUR NOSE IN A GOOD BOOK
- ANCHOR YOURSELF IN A GOOD BOOK
- CUT YOUR TEETH ON A GOOD BOOK

CURL UP WITH A GOOD BOOK

11

DESIGN A SPACE-AGE LIBRARY
11 and up

DISCUSS WITH YOUR TEACHER THE IMPACT OF COMPUTERS ON INFORMATION STORAGE

- WILL HOME COMPUTERS SUPERSEDE LIBRARIES?
- WILL ROBOTS REPLACE LIBRARIANS?
- WILL MICROFICHE, MICROFILM, VIDEO, COMPUTER DISC REPLACE PAPER?

Choose:
DRAW A PLAN / MAKE A MODEL OR DIORAMA / WRITE A USER-GUIDE TO THE NEW-AGE LIBRARY

12

Right, Kids, Hitchcock's been knocked out of fifth place by Seuss, Cleary's still the favourite, with Milligan out of the running and Hoban coming on fast

AUTHORS' TOP TEN
8 and up

ONCE A TERM THE CLASS DISC JOCKEY TAKES VOTES ON THE CURRENT TOP TEN AUTHORS. THE DJ SELECTS TEN HELPERS. EACH TAKES ONE AUTHOR AND, USING THE FICTION AUTHOR FILE OF THE LIBRARY CATALOGUE, LISTS THE TITLES WRITTEN BY THAT AUTHOR THAT THE SCHOOL LIBRARY OWNS.

AUTHOR	RATING	TITLES IN SCHOOL LIBRARY
Beverly CLEARY	1	Henry Huggins / Ramona the pest / Ribsey and her motorcycle.
Roald DAHL	2	Charlie & the chocolate factory / Charlie & the great glass elevator
Willard PRICE	3	Underwater adventure / Arctic adventure / ...
Bill PEET	4	...
Dr SEUSS	5	Cat in the hat
Ray BRIGGS	6	Father Christmas / Fungus the Bogeyman
J. FITZGERALD	7	The great Brain
E.B. WHITE	8	Charlotte's web.
D. SOBOL	9	Encyclopaedia Brown.
C.S. LEWIS	10	Magician's Nephew

PS Good opportunity to visit the Public Library to see if they have any more titles by these authors.

PPS Write to school library Service to ask if they have any more titles.

13 FICTION DETECTIVE GAME

9 AND UP

THE CLASS IS DIVIDED IN HALF
EACH HALF PREPARES A SET OF FICTION QUESTION
CARDS LIKE THE ONES ILLUSTRATED.
THE CARDS ARE SWAPPED AND THE
GAME IS PLAYED LIKE A RELAY RACE.
ONE CHILD IS APPOINTED DIRECTOR.
THE FIRST PERSON FROM EACH TEAM IS
HANDED A CARD AND RUSHES TO THE
CATALOGUE OR SHELVES TO FIND THE ANSWER.
THE DIRECTOR GIVES 10 POINTS FOR EACH
CORRECT ANSWER, -5 PENALTY POINTS FOR
EACH INCORRECT ANSWER.
(THE DIRECTOR HAS THE ANSWERS)

IS "THE SILVER SWORD" A NON-FICTION BOOK ABOUT WEAPONS? WHO WROTE IT?

WHO WROTE "THE GHOST OF THOMAS KEMPE"?

WHAT IS THE NAME OF CLIVE KING'S MOST FAMOUS FICTIONAL CHARACTER?

HOW MANY BOOKS BY ROALD DAHL ARE THERE IN OUR LIBRARY?

IN WHICH COUNTRY DOES "THE OWL SERVICE" TAKE PLACE?

WHAT SORT OF BOOKS DOES SUSAN COOPER WRITE? ADVENTURE? GHOST STORIES? FANTASY?

WHAT WAS THE NAME OF THE FAMILY INVENTED BY THE AUTHOR TOVE JANSSON?

FATTYPUFFS AND ---

GIVE THE NAME OF AN AUTHOR WHO WROTE MONSTER STORIES. HIS NAME IS MAY--

GIVE THE NAME OF A FICTION TITLE WHICH BEGINS "I AM ...."

WAS "THE LIGHTHOUSEKEEPER'S LUNCH" WRITTEN BY DAVID ARMITAGE?

14 ALPHABETICAL SURNAMES

8 and up

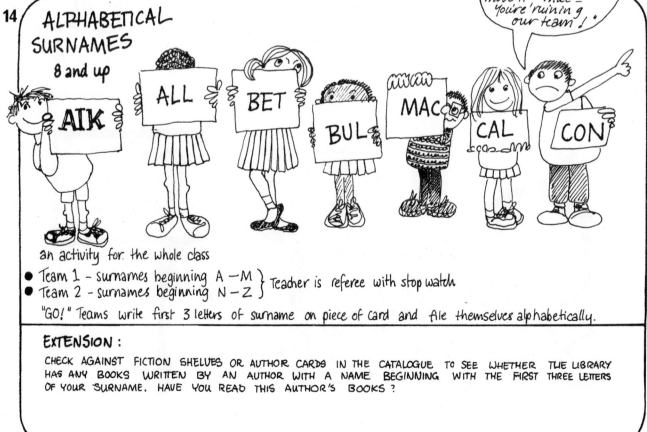

"move it Mac - you're ruining our team!"

an activity for the whole class

- Team 1 - surnames beginning A − M } Teacher is referee with stop watch
- Team 2 - surnames beginning N − Z

"GO!" Teams write first 3 letters of surname on piece of card and file themselves alphabetically.

EXTENSION:

CHECK AGAINST FICTION SHELVES OR AUTHOR CARDS IN THE CATALOGUE TO SEE WHETHER THE LIBRARY HAS ANY BOOKS WRITTEN BY AN AUTHOR WITH A NAME BEGINNING WITH THE FIRST THREE LETTERS OF YOUR SURNAME. HAVE YOU READ THIS AUTHOR'S BOOKS?

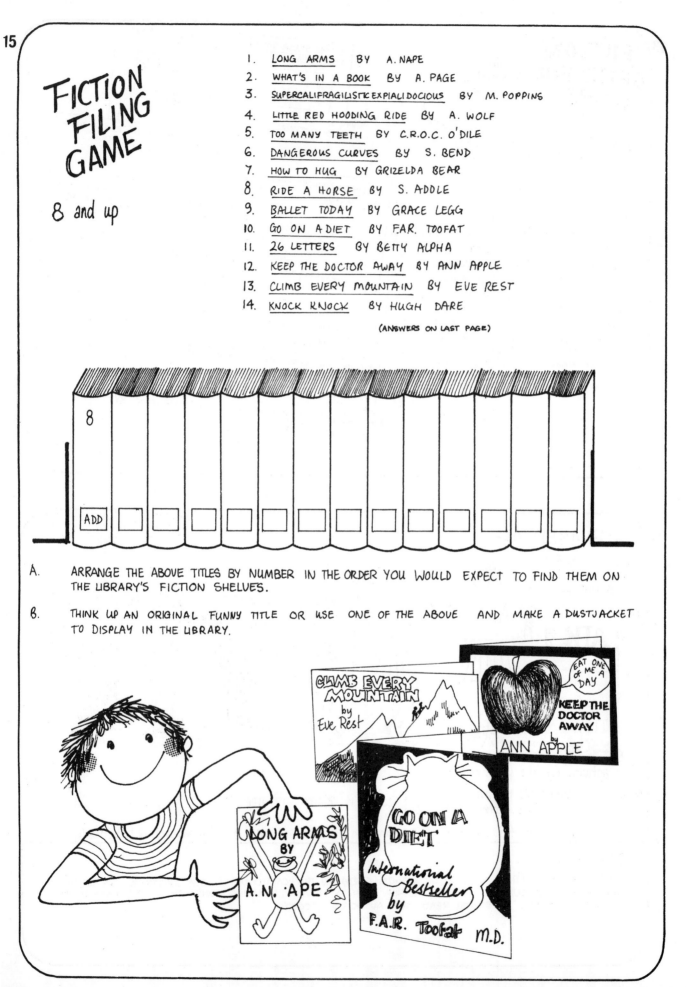

FICTION FILING GAME

8 and up

1. <u>LONG ARMS</u>   BY   A. NAPE
2. <u>WHAT'S IN A BOOK</u>   BY   A. PAGE
3. <u>SUPERCALIFRAGILISTIC EXPIALIDOCIOUS</u>   BY   M. POPPINS
4. <u>LITTLE RED HOODING RIDE</u>   BY   A. WOLF
5. <u>TOO MANY TEETH</u>   BY   C.R.O.C. O'DILE
6. <u>DANGEROUS CURVES</u>   BY   S. BEND
7. <u>HOW TO HUG</u>   BY GRIZELDA BEAR
8. <u>RIDE A HORSE</u>   BY   S. ADDLE
9. <u>BALLET TODAY</u>   BY   GRACE LEGG
10. <u>GO ON A DIET</u>   BY   F.A.R. TOOFAT
11. <u>26 LETTERS</u>   BY   BETTY ALPHA
12. <u>KEEP THE DOCTOR AWAY</u>   BY ANN APPLE
13. <u>CLIMB EVERY MOUNTAIN</u>   BY   EVE REST
14. <u>KNOCK KNOCK</u>   BY HUGH DARE

(ANSWERS ON LAST PAGE)

A.   ARRANGE THE ABOVE TITLES BY NUMBER IN THE ORDER YOU WOULD EXPECT TO FIND THEM ON THE LIBRARY'S FICTION SHELVES.

B.   THINK UP AN ORIGINAL FUNNY TITLE OR USE ONE OF THE ABOVE AND MAKE A DUSTJACKET TO DISPLAY IN THE LIBRARY.

THE CASE OF THE BORING BOOK

9 and up

MLUD, I ACCUSE THIS BOOK OF BEING BORING, HAVING NO OBVIOUS PLOT, CHARACTER DEVELOPMENT OR THEME.. IT IS FULL OF BIG WORDS, LONG SENTENCES, TOO MANY DESCRIPTIONS OF LANDSCAPE AND NOT ENOUGH ACTION. IT IS OLD AND SMELLY.

MLUD, AS THE COUNSEL FOR THE DEFENCE OF THIS INNOCENT BOOK I MUST PROTEST. THIS BOOK MIGHT NOT BE WRITTEN IN THE DRAMATIC LANGUAGE OF A TV SERIAL, BUT IT REPRESENTS HISTORY— HOW THE WORLD WAS, HOW LANGUAGE WAS. HOW CAN THE PAST BE BORING? THE AUTHOR WAS A LEGEND IN HIS TIME.

DISCUSS WITH YOUR TEACHER WHAT MAKES A BOOK EXCITING AND WHAT MAKES A BOOK DEADLY BORING.

WORK WITH A FRIEND AND TRY TO FIND ONE REALLY DULL, BORING FICTION BOOK ON THE LIBRARY SHELVES.

CHOOSE TWO CHILDREN AS PROSECUTION TO GIVE ALL THE BAD FEATURES OF THE BOOK.

CHOOSE TWO CHILDREN AS THE DEFENCE TO DEFEND ALL THE BOOK'S GOOD FEATURES.

PROSECUTION, DEFENCE AND JUDGE (TEACHER) MUST READ THE BOOK! JUDGE MAY APPOINT JURY.

JUDGE: WEIGHS UP THE EVIDENCE FOR AND AGAINST THE BOOK TO DECIDE WHETHER OR NOT ITS WORTH HAVING IN THE SCHOOL LIBRARY.

IF THE BOOK IS FOUND GUILTY, IT IS SENTENCED TO WEEDING AND WITHDRAWAL.

DEFENCE MAY INSTITUTE AN APPEAL ON BEHALF OF THE BOOK.

FICTION CARDS

all ages

WORK WITH A GROUP OF FRIENDS TO RECORD YOUR FAVOURITE BOOKS ON DECORATED FICTION TOPIC CARDS.

WHEN YOU'VE FILLED ALL THE TITLE SLOTS YOU CAN STAPLE THE SHEETS INTO A "RECOMMENDED BOOKS" BOOKLIST.

READERS WHO ENJOY SCIENCE FICTION, ADVENTURE, HORSE STORIES etc COULD ALSO MAKE AUTHOR CARDS

adventure authors

WILLARD PRICE
DONALD SOBOL
JAY WILLIAMS AND RAYMOND ABRASHKIN
BRUCE CARTER
ROY BROWN
E.W. HILDICK
BERNARD ASHLEY
NICHOLAS FISK

bated breath stories
FUR AND FEATHER STORIES
OUT OF THIS WORLD
Freaky Family Stories

FUNNY HA HA's

NAME	AUTHOR	TITLE	RATING
Ann Brown	YEOMAN, J & BLAKE, Q	The wild washerwoman	★★★★
Jeff Jones	ROCKWELL, Thomas	How to eat fried worms	★★★★
Hilary Herford	WILLIAMS and ABRASHKIN	Danny Dunn and the homework machine	★★★★
Jocelyn Fine	BROWN, Jeff	Flat Stanley	★★★★★
Harry Jones	AHLBERG, Janet & Allan	Funnybones	★★★
Karen Davies	AHLBERG, Janet & Allan	Burglar Bill	★★★★
Anne Fisk	HUTCHINS, Pat	The tale of Thomas Mead	★★★
Penny Hooper	HOBAN, Russell	ACE DRAGON LTD	★★★
Graham Turner	MAHY, Margaret	The great-piratical rumbustification	★★★★
Gwenda Poole	WELLS, Rosemary	Benjamin and Tulip	★★★★
Ann Catley	HOBAN, R and BLAKE, Q	How Tom beat Captain Najork and his hired sportsmen	★★★★★
Alan Hyborn	KEMP, Gene	The turbulent term of Tyke Tiler	★★★★

FICTION AUCTION

AND WHAT AM I OFFERED FOR THIS AMAZING ADVENTURE STORY ... THE SORT OF BOOK THAT MAKES YOUR BLOOD RUN COLD AND YOUR HEART PUMP FAST. **FROZEN FIRE** IS MORE THAN AN ADVENTURE. IT'S A GRIPPING ACCOUNT OF SURVIVAL AGAINST INCREDIBLE ODDS. IF YOU WANT TO KNOW WHAT IT FEELS LIKE TO BE ALONE AND LOST A MILLION MILES FROM ANYWHERE, BID FOR THIS BOOK **NOW!**

TWO BOOKITS?

Pssssst — I've read it — he's exaggerating

AUCTIONEER

AUCTIONEERS (NOT MORE THAN 10) ARE CHOSEN IN ADVANCE. THEY GET THE CHANCE TO READ GOOD, EXCITING, NEW FICTION BOOKS. EACH AUCTIONEER FILLS IN AN AUCTION ANALYSIS SHEET. BEFORE THE AUCTION THE AUDIENCE IS GIVEN TOKENS CALLED BOOKITS. (SAY 20 EACH) THE AUCTIONEERS PRESENT THEIR AUCTIONEERING SALES BLURB AND THE AUDIENCE BIDS. THE WINNING BIDDER GETS FIRST CHANCE TO READ THE BOOK, ETC.

AUCTION ANALYSIS

AUTHOR: _____

TITLE: _____

STRONG POINTS: INTERESTING? EXCITING, GRIPPING, THRILLING, TENSE? SAD? FUNNY? WARM & HAPPY? MYSTERIOUS? SCARY? CREEPY?
_____
_____

WEAK POINTS: TOO LONG? TOO MUCH DESCRIPTION / NOT ENOUGH ACTION? DIFFICULT LANGUAGE? TAKES TOO LONG TO GET INTO? BORING? DULL?
_____

AUCTIONEER'S SALES BLURB _____
_____
_____
_____
_____
_____
_____
_____
_____

SPACE AGE reading records

RECORDS WHICH CAN BE MADE SMALL, IF INDIVIDUAL, OR REALLY BIG FOR A SPECTACULAR CLASS RECORD. GROUP OR INDIVIDUAL READING LOOKS GREAT IF GOLD OR SILVER CARD IS USED AND THE ROCKET OR SPACESHIP IS MOUNTED ON BLACK PAPER SPRINKLED WITH STARS.

THE ROCKET IS MADE BY TAKING A RECTANGULAR STRIP OF CARDBOARD, CUTTING OUT A TRIANGLE AND LOTS OF BOXES THE SAME WIDTH AS THE STRIP. STARTING AT THE TOP, STAPLE THE TRIANGLE THEN STAPLE THE BOXES ONTO THE STRIP BASE STAPLE EACH ONE AT THE SIDE AND BASE OVERLAP EACH BOX SLIGHTLY TO MAKE A POCKET.

Alien Invader mask!!

DRAW A CIRCLE AND CUT IT IN HALF FOR THE SPACECRAFT. FOLD A RECTANGULAR STRIP OF CARD IN HALF TO MAKE A POCKET FOR THE MARTIANS TO STAND IN. ATTACH LEGS AND CIRCLES OR MARGARINE LIDS FOR LANDING PADS

HOBAN, RUSSELL
Arthur's new power.
★ ★ ★

FLEISCHMAN, S.I.D.
Goodbye to the purple sage
★ ★ ★ ★

MAKE AN ASTRONAUT FOR EACH BOOK YOU READ. PUT AUTHOR/TITLE AND STAR RATING ONTO YOUR ASTRONAUT AND PUT HIM INTO ONE OF THE POCKETS

MAKE MARTIANS FOR THE ALIEN INVADER CRAFT. ANTENNAE AND ARMS MADE OUT OF RUBBER BANDS LOOK GOOD. REMEMBER AUTHOR/ TITLE AND STAR RATING FOR YOUR MINI BOOK REVIEW. TRY SOME FUN MARTIANS - GREEN, PINK, PURPLE, TWO-HEADED, THREE-EYED, FIVE-ARMED.

Windsurfer Reading Records

A GROUP READING RECORD FOR THE WHOLE CLASS TO MAKE

The great Gilly Hopkins by Katherine Paterson

★★★★★

Read by Ann Jones

MAKE WINDSURFERS OR YACHTS OUT OF A TRIANGLE OF COLOURED PAPER OR CARD. WHEN YOU HAVE FINISHED A BOOK, ADD AUTHOR/TITLE AND STAR RATING. THEN STAPLE THE SAIL ONTO A SHEET OF BLUE CARD, MARKED INTO READING WAVES. GET YOUR FRIENDS TO DO THE SAME AND SEE WHICH WAVE FILLS UP FIRST.

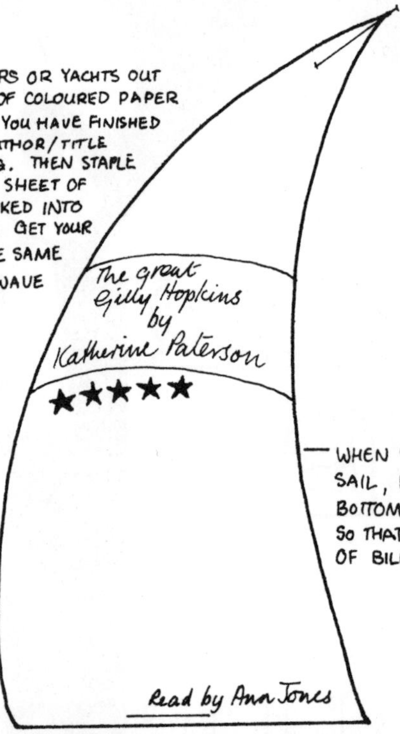

The great Gilly Hopkins by Katherine Paterson

★★★★★

Read by Ann Jones

WHEN YOU STAPLE YOUR SAIL, PUSH TOP AND BOTTOM TOGETHER SLIGHTLY SO THAT YOU GET THE EFFECT OF BILLOWING.

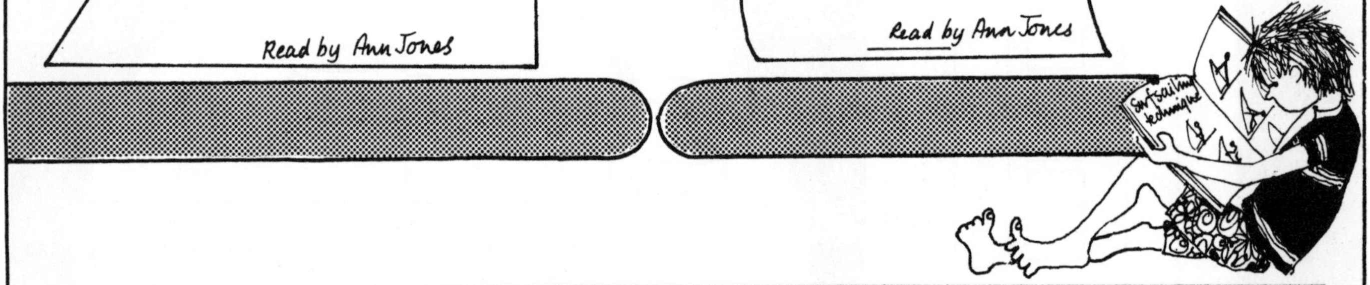

ADVENTURE

HUMOUR

WAR STORIES

ANIMAL

SCIENCE FICTION

ROOM 4 : WINDSURFERS' GUIDE TO THE BEST READING WAVES

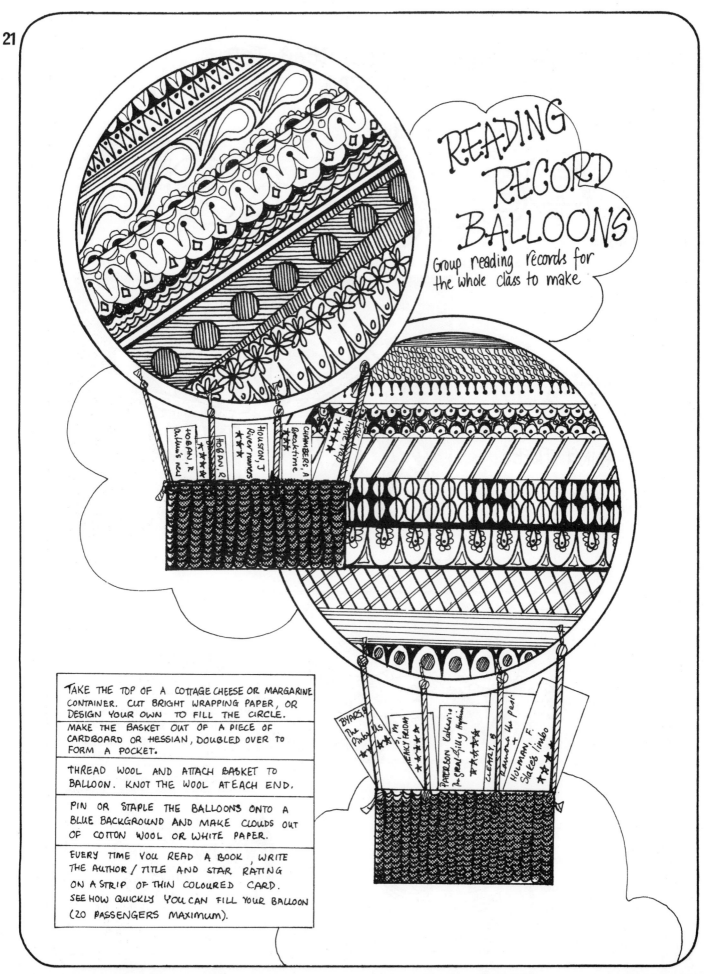

READING RECORD BALLOONS

Group reading records for the whole class to make

TAKE THE TOP OF A COTTAGE CHEESE OR MARGARINE CONTAINER. CUT BRIGHT WRAPPING PAPER, OR DESIGN YOUR OWN TO FILL THE CIRCLE.

MAKE THE BASKET OUT OF A PIECE OF CARDBOARD OR HESSIAN, DOUBLED OVER TO FORM A POCKET.

THREAD WOOL AND ATTACH BASKET TO BALLOON. KNOT THE WOOL AT EACH END.

PIN OR STAPLE THE BALLOONS ONTO A BLUE BACKGROUND AND MAKE CLOUDS OUT OF COTTON WOOL OR WHITE PAPER.

EVERY TIME YOU READ A BOOK, WRITE THE AUTHOR / TITLE AND STAR RATING ON A STRIP OF THIN COLOURED CARD.
SEE HOW QUICKLY YOU CAN FILL YOUR BALLOON (20 PASSENGERS MAXIMUM).

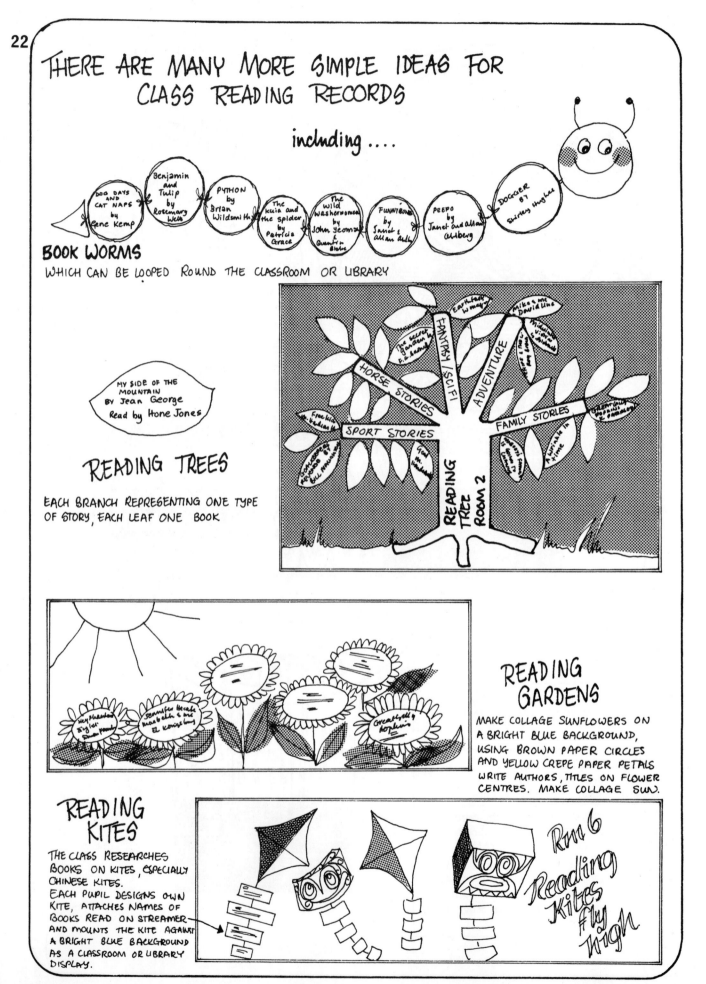

THERE ARE MANY MORE SIMPLE IDEAS FOR CLASS READING RECORDS

including ....

Dog Days and Cat Naps by Gene Kemp

Benjamin and Tulip by Rosemary Wells

Python by Brian Wildsmith

The Kuia and the Spider by Patricia Grace

The Wild Washerwomen by John Yeoman & Quentin Blake

Funnybones by Janet & Allan Ahlberg

Peepo by Janet and Allan Ahlberg

Dogger by Shirley Hughes

BOOK WORMS

WHICH CAN BE LOOPED ROUND THE CLASSROOM OR LIBRARY

MY SIDE OF THE MOUNTAIN BY Jean George Read by Hone Jones

READING TREES

EACH BRANCH REPRESENTING ONE TYPE OF STORY, EACH LEAF ONE BOOK

FANTASY/SCI FI
HORSE STORIES
ADVENTURE
SPORT STORIES
FAMILY STORIES

READING TREE Room 2

READING GARDENS

MAKE COLLAGE SUNFLOWERS ON A BRIGHT BLUE BACKGROUND, USING BROWN PAPER CIRCLES AND YELLOW CREPE PAPER PETALS WRITE AUTHORS, TITLES ON FLOWER CENTRES. MAKE COLLAGE SUN.

READING KITES

THE CLASS RESEARCHES BOOKS ON KITES, ESPECIALLY CHINESE KITES.
EACH PUPIL DESIGNS OWN KITE, ATTACHES NAMES OF BOOKS READ ON STREAMER AND MOUNTS THE KITE AGAINST A BRIGHT BLUE BACKGROUND AS A CLASSROOM OR LIBRARY DISPLAY.

Rm 6 Reading Kites Fly High

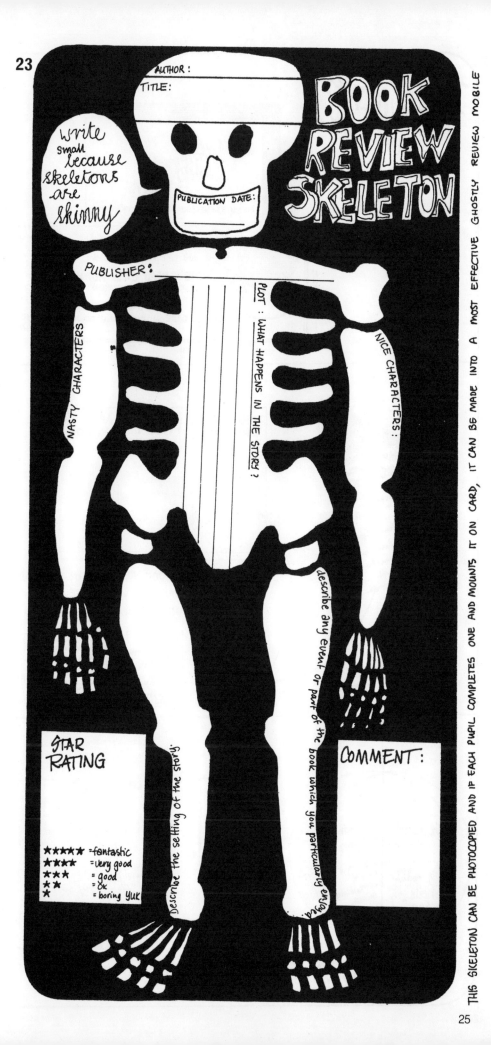

BOOK REVIEWS
THE FUN WAY

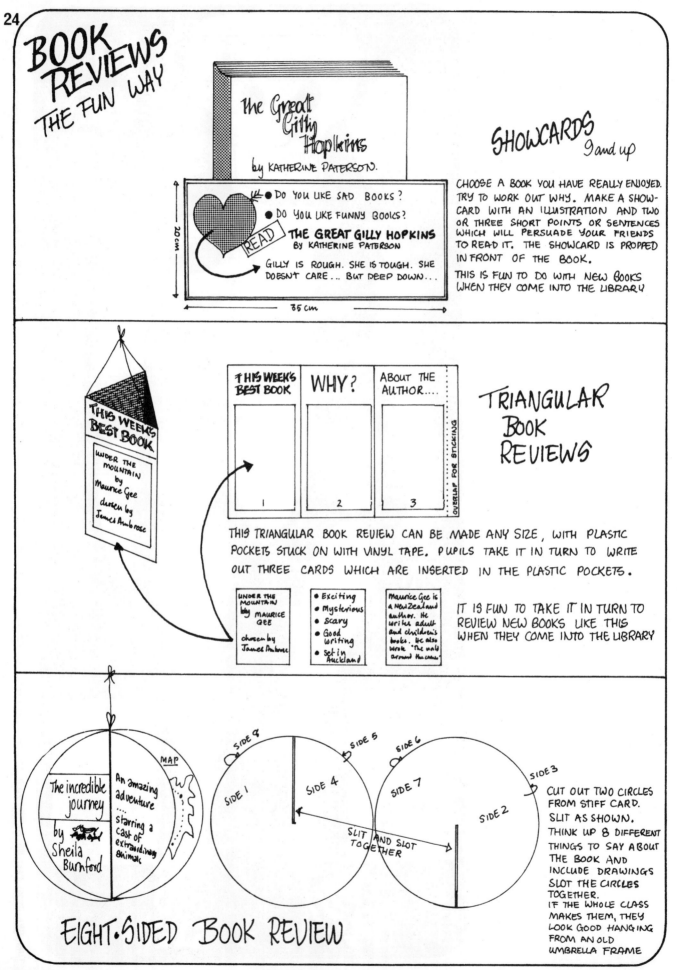

The Great Gilly Hopkins
by KATHERINE PATERSON.

● DO YOU LIKE SAD BOOKS?
● DO YOU LIKE FUNNY BOOKS?

READ **THE GREAT GILLY HOPKINS**
BY KATHERINE PATERSON

GILLY IS ROUGH. SHE IS TOUGH. SHE
DOESN'T CARE... BUT DEEP DOWN...

20cm

35 cm

SHOWCARDS 9 and up

CHOOSE A BOOK YOU HAVE REALLY ENJOYED.
TRY TO WORK OUT WHY. MAKE A SHOW-
CARD WITH AN ILLUSTRATION AND TWO
OR THREE SHORT POINTS OR SENTENCES
WHICH WILL PERSUADE YOUR FRIENDS
TO READ IT. THE SHOWCARD IS PROPPED
IN FRONT OF THE BOOK.

THIS IS FUN TO DO WITH NEW BOOKS
WHEN THEY COME INTO THE LIBRARY

THIS WEEK'S BEST BOOK

UNDER THE MOUNTAIN
by Maurice Gee
chosen by James Ambrose

THIS WEEK'S BEST BOOK | WHY? | ABOUT THE AUTHOR....

1   2   3

OVERLAP FOR STICKING

TRIANGULAR BOOK REVIEWS

THIS TRIANGULAR BOOK REVIEW CAN BE MADE ANY SIZE, WITH PLASTIC
POCKETS STUCK ON WITH VINYL TAPE. PUPILS TAKE IT IN TURN TO WRITE
OUT THREE CARDS WHICH ARE INSERTED IN THE PLASTIC POCKETS.

UNDER THE MOUNTAIN
by MAURICE GEE

chosen by James Ambrose

● Exciting
● Mysterious
● Scary
● Good Writing
● Set in Auckland

Maurice Gee is a New Zealand author. He writes adult and children's books. He also wrote "The walk around the lake"

IT IS FUN TO TAKE IT IN TURN TO
REVIEW NEW BOOKS LIKE THIS
WHEN THEY COME INTO THE LIBRARY

The incredible journey
by Sheila Burnford

An amazing adventure .... starring a cast of extraordinary animals

MAP

SIDE 8   SIDE 5   SIDE 6

SIDE 1   SIDE 4   SIDE 7   SIDE 3

SLIT AND SLOT TOGETHER   SIDE 2

CUT OUT TWO CIRCLES
FROM STIFF CARD.
SLIT AS SHOWN.
THINK UP 8 DIFFERENT
THINGS TO SAY ABOUT
THE BOOK AND
INCLUDE DRAWINGS
SLOT THE CIRCLES
TOGETHER.
IF THE WHOLE CLASS
MAKES THEM, THEY
LOOK GOOD HANGING
FROM AN OLD
UMBRELLA FRAME

EIGHT-SIDED BOOK REVIEW

AUTHORS 8 and up

COMPLETE THIS **AUTHOR PROFILE** FOR YOUR FAVOURITE AUTHOR:

AUTHOR'S NAME _____

TITLES OF BOOKS
IN SCHOOL LIBRARY _____

_____

_____

_____

TITLES BORROWED FROM _____
SCHOOL LIBRARY SERVICE/
PUBLIC LIBRARY / FRIENDS _____

ABOUT THE **AUTHOR'S LIFE**:

BORN WHEN? _____ WHERE? _____

MARRIED? _____ CHILDREN? _____

HAS SHE/HE ALWAYS BEEN AN AUTHOR? OTHER JOBS?

_____

_____

REMARKS: _____

_____

_____

◄ PICTURE OF THE AUTHOR OR DRAWING OF ONE
OF THE CHARACTERS OR EVENTS FROM HER/HIS BOOKS

AUTHOR
PROFILES
COMPILED BY RM 8
1983

AUTHOR PROFILE
SHEETS CAN BE MADE
INTO AUTHOR CHARTS
(ILLUSTRATED WITH BOOK CHARACTERS)
OR BOUND INTO A BOOK
(see activity 42) OR PASTED
ONTO COLOURED CIRCLES AND
SQUARES AND USED AS AN
UMBRELLA MOBILE

PAT
HUTCHINS

ROALD DAHL

HUGHES

ROY BROWN

JILL PATON WALSH
TITLES

GOODIES and BADDIES IN FICTION

GOODIES GALAXY

BADDIES BRIGADE

AUTHOR _____

TITLE _____

I like _____ because _____

AUTHOR _____

TITLE _____

I don't like _____ because _____

AUTHOR _____

TITLE _____

I like _____ because _____

AUTHOR _____

TITLE _____

I don't like _____ because _____

AUTHOR _____

TITLE _____

I like _____ because _____

AUTHOR _____

TITLE _____

I don't like _____ because _____

AUTHOR _____

TITLE _____

I like _____ because _____

AUTHOR _____

TITLE _____

I don't like _____ because _____

AUTHOR _____

TITLE _____

I like _____ because _____

AUTHOR _____

TITLE _____

I don't like _____ because _____

NORTON, Andre
  Postmarked the stars.   Gollancz, 1971.

◄ FICTION AUTHOR CARD

FICTION TITLE CARD

          Postmarked the stars.
          NORTON, Andre

▼

          STARS   523.1

523.1

  BRANLEY, Franklin M
    A book of outer space for you.   Crowell,
  1970.

▲ SUBJECT INDEX CARD

◄ CLASSIFIED CARD

NON·FICTION

Hitch hiker's guide to the Catalogue

Q: HOW WOULD YOU FIND OUT THE DEWEY NUMBER OF ANY SUBJECT ?

A : _____

Q: HOW WOULD YOU FIND OUT WHO WROTE CHARLIE AND THE CHOCOLATE FACTORY ?

A : _____

Q: HOW WOULD YOU FIND OUT HOW MANY BOOKS ON HORSE RIDING YOUR LIBRARY OWNS ?

A : _____

Q HOW WOULD YOU FIND OUT HOW MANY BOOKS BY ROALD DAHL YOUR LIBRARY OWNS ?

A : _____

(ANSWERS ON LAST PAGE)

MR DEWEY'S INVENTION

Mr and Mrs Dewey loved reading. They loved reading so much that they could not bear the thought of giving away any of their hundreds and hundreds of books. When their ten children grew up and left home, they had even more time for reading and even more room for books. Suddenly there were thousands and thousands of books filling every room, stacked in piles on the stairs, stacked in boxes, stacked under beds, on top of beds, on top of tables, chairs, wardrobes.

Mrs Dewey owned a motorbike and loved nothing more than tinkering and tonkering in the engine with the help of a motorcycle maintenance manual — *when* she could find one! One day Mrs Dewey looked in vain for her favourite book *Nuts and bolts of supercycles*. She hunted high and low through stacks, piles, crates, shelves and boxes of books, up stepladders and down on her hands and knees. She called Mr Dewey from the kitchen where he was baking Deweylova (he could not find the recipe for Pavlova).

"Dewey dear," said Mrs Dewey, "if you're so good at inventing recipes, why don't you invent a recipe for instant book-finding?"

"What a good idea, dear," said Mr Dewey, And he did!

He decided to clear every book out of the house and put them in the garage while he sorted them into categories or subjects. This took him a whole week. Mrs Dewey had to take over the kitchen duties. This did not please her one little bit! Mr Dewey's plan took shape gradually, and one day it was ready. He borrowed his neighbour's wheelbarrow, and barrowload by barrowload he trundled the books inside again.

100   Mr Dewey was very proud of his shiny bald head, and very proud of the work that went on inside it. He decided that all his books on thinking, on **Philosophy** and **Psychology** and **Information** should go in the first room. By Saturday night the room was full.

200   Mr Dewey found that he owned so many books on people's **Beliefs** and **Religions** and **Mythologies** that they needed a room to themselves. He thought that it was appropriate to move them on Sunday. So he did.

300 On Monday morning Mr Dewey went out to do the weekly shopping. This made him realise that there was more to life than just thinking and believing. There were people, streets and streets full of people, talking, shopping, posting letters, driving in cars and buses, going to work and to school. When he got home, Mr Dewey searched the garage for books on the **Community** — on trade, commerce, politics, government, welfare, education, law and transport. He also remembered how communities record their lore and legends, in fairy tales and folk tales. He loved these books. They made him feel so old, and so young. He was exhausted so he sat in the wheelbarrow, pulled his hat over his eyes and had a snooze. When he woke up he remembered what he had forgotten. He had forgotten there are bad things about communities too. So he hunted for all the books on crime and pollution and warfare and reluctantly made room for them.

400 Mr Dewey loved cooking. Even more than cooking he loved talking. He owned many dictionaries, grammars and thesauri. After the exhausting Monday he has spent moving all the community books, he decided to give himself a treat, taking the whole of Tuesday to move his **Language** books, and giving them their own room so that the words would have lots of room to fly around. He sang antonyms and synonyms softly to himself all day.

500 Mrs Dewey thought he was crazy. "Dewey darling", she said, "if I didn't take you out for rides on my motorbike you'd spend your life talking to yourself in the kitchen! What about the world outside? What about the sea, stars, land, mountains, molehills, volcanoes, rocks and rivers? What about the insects and birds and animals and plants and trees and dinosaurs and reptiles and tuataras and amphibians? What about the laws that govern nature and numbers — **Science**? What about mathematics, astronomy, physics, chemistry, geology, palaeontology, biology, botany, zoology?"

"That's nice, dear," replied Mr Dewey. "They all end in 'ics' or 'y'. I'll keep them all together."

And he did, in the fifth room, on Wednesday.

600 "Fair enough, Dewey dear," said Mrs Dewey. "But is all that more important than finding my motorbike manual?"

"No dear," replied Mr Dewey meekly. "You'll have a whole shelf in the next room." And she did! In went technology and mechanical repairs and machines and electronics and that sort of thing.

"Splendid, ducky," said Mrs Dewey, "but don't forget that the human body is the most amazing machine of all."
So in went the books on the
human body!

"And now comes MY hobby," said Mr Dewey, "yummy food and scrumptious cooking, and while I'm at it I'll shove in all the books on how food is grown and farmed and harvested and processed. In fact, I'll put in anything that is nature adapted by people for their own purposes — even dogs and cats and pets. I'll put in anything that people invent, engineer, grow, manufacture, process, build. I'll call this room **Applied Science** and **Technology**."

"Good for you, dear," said Mrs Dewey. "I like that. It has a nice scientific ring to it."

By the time he had worked out the arrangement of the sixth room it was late on Thursday night.

700 "I hope you're not going to work all weekend, Dewey dear," said Mrs Dewey.

"No, dearest," said Mr Dewey. "Tomorrow I'm going to invent **Sport** and **Recreation**."

And he did. He got out all his favourite books on singing and dancing and playing the bagpipes, and sang and danced and bagpiped like crazy till the neighbours complained. Then he got out his books on drawing and painting and modelling and making kites and puppets, and he drew and painted and sculpted and crafted and kited and puppeted till his wife complained. "You need to get outside and get some fresh air, Dewey dear," Mrs Dewey exclaimed.

"Yes dear," said Mr Dewey, picking up his rugby books and tennis books and soccer books and golf, skating, mountaineering, skiing, sailing, swimming and surfing books. "Now I won't be bored this weekend, dear."

"That's nice, dear, but will you have time for Shakespeare?" asked Mrs Dewey.

"I'll do him tomorrow," replied Mr Dewey. And he did!

800   On Saturday he shifted Shakespeare, along with plays, poetry and funny verse and he enjoyed himself very much, humming, "lovely lovely **Literature**" under his breath all day.

900   On Sunday he scratched his head and puzzled over the huge pile of books that remained. "Of course … the rest of the world … how they live now … how they lived long ago …," And into room 9 went **Geography** and **History** and **Biography**.

000   "That's all!" Dewey announced proudly to his wife on Sunday night.

"Oh no it isn't," she replied. "There are still great piles of books outside on every topic imaginable, and you've only used nine rooms."

"But that's the problem, Mrs Dewey, dearest," said Mr Dewey. "The books that are left are on every topic imaginable and I don't know what to do with them."

"Dewey, my genius," Mrs Dewey replied, "that's why you need a whole room for books like encyclopaedias which cover lots of subjects and topics. Now hurry along, dear, or you won't have time to make dinner, and I'm going out on my motorbike."

With a big sigh, Dewey did!

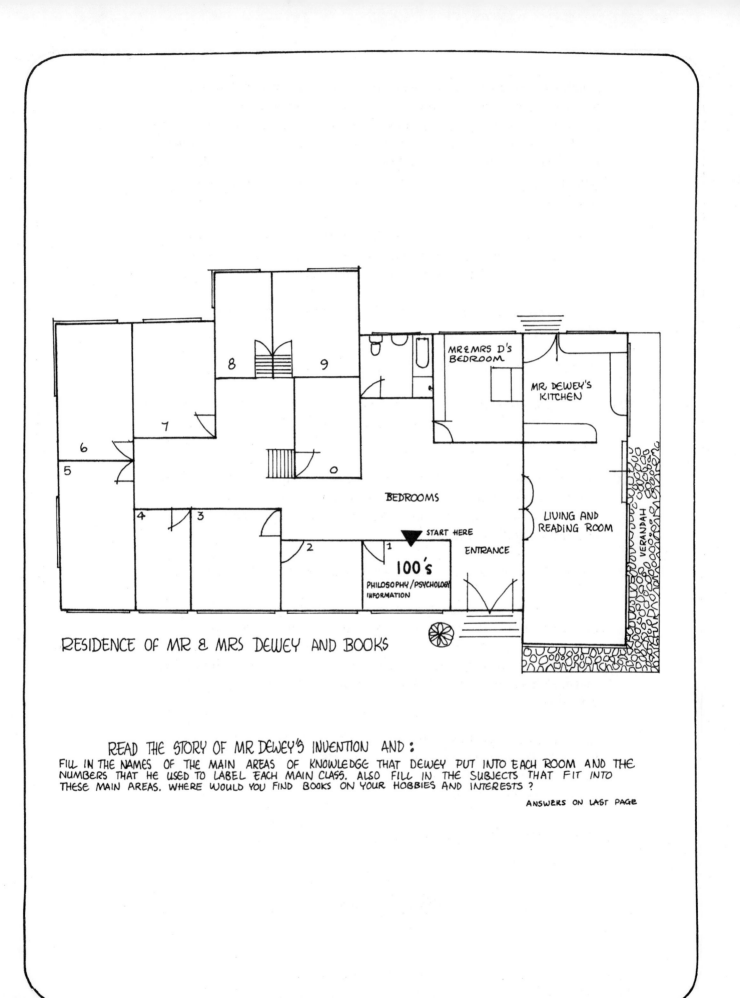

RESIDENCE OF MR & MRS DEWEY AND BOOKS

READ THE STORY OF MR DEWEY'S INVENTION AND:
FILL IN THE NAMES OF THE MAIN AREAS OF KNOWLEDGE THAT DEWEY PUT INTO EACH ROOM AND THE
NUMBERS THAT HE USED TO LABEL EACH MAIN CLASS. ALSO FILL IN THE SUBJECTS THAT FIT INTO
THESE MAIN AREAS. WHERE WOULD YOU FIND BOOKS ON YOUR HOBBIES AND INTERESTS?

ANSWERS ON LAST PAGE

8 - 10

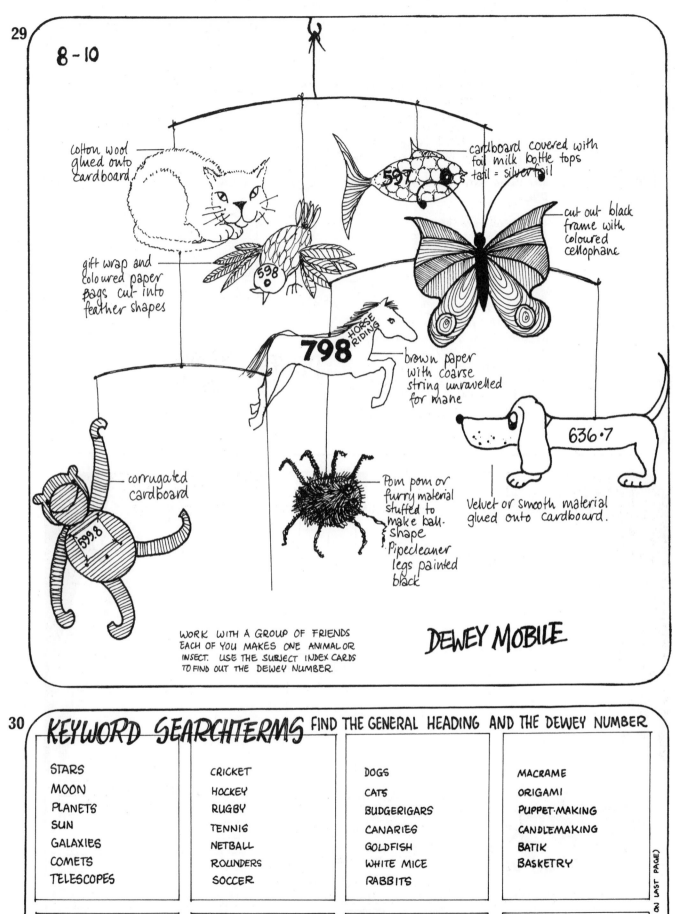

cotton wool glued onto cardboard

cardboard covered with foil milk bottle tops tail = silver foil

597

598

cut out black frame with coloured cellophane

gift wrap and coloured paper bags cut into feather shapes

798 HORSE RIDING

brown paper with coarse string unravelled for mane

636·7

corrugated cardboard

599·8

Pom pom or furry material stuffed to make ball shape. Pipecleaner legs painted black

Velvet or smooth material glued onto cardboard.

WORK WITH A GROUP OF FRIENDS EACH OF YOU MAKES ONE ANIMAL OR INSECT. USE THE SUBJECT INDEX CARDS TO FIND OUT THE DEWEY NUMBER.

DEWEY MOBILE

KEYWORD SEARCHTERMS   FIND THE GENERAL HEADING AND THE DEWEY NUMBER

STARS	CRICKET	DOGS	MACRAME
MOON	HOCKEY	CATS	ORIGAMI
PLANETS	RUGBY	BUDGERIGARS	PUPPET·MAKING
SUN	TENNIS	CANARIES	CANDLEMAKING
GALAXIES	NETBALL	GOLDFISH	BATIK
COMETS	ROUNDERS	WHITE MICE	BASKETRY
TELESCOPES	SOCCER	RABBITS	

(ANSWERS ON LAST PAGE)

KEYWORD: ASTRONOMY

DEWEY NO: 523

KEYWORD:

DEWEY NO:

KEYWORD:

DEWEY NO:

KEYWORD:

DEWEY NO:

Work with your friends. Choose a broad subject like sport.
Think of all the activities that come under the heading of
'sport'. Go through old magazines, pamphlets, advertising
to find appropriate pictures to illustrate each sport.
Use old margarine lids to frame your cut-out pictures.

Then use the SUBJECT INDEX cards to
find the Dewey number and
write it on the reverse (white)
side using spirit-based felt tip
pens.

Using needle and thread string
the tops together to make a
Sporting Dewey Mobile

Other good subjects include THE SEA
(ships/fish/crabs/ocean currents/pirates/submarines/
sea mammals/fishing (sport)/fishing (commercial) etc.;
TRANSPORT (steam ships/road/rail/air/balloon/
motorcycle/electric cars/ox carts/horse-drawn/
dog sleds/skis/sleds/sedan chair/camel/elephant etc.)
HOBBIES AND INTERESTS (collecting/craftwork/
puppetry/drawing/print making/photography/cooking etc.)

DEWEY MOBILE MARK II

9 and up

DEWEY LOCATER

10 and up

all these aspects of fishing will
be found in different areas
of Dewey. See if you can work
out roughly where you'd find
books on these topics

(ANSWERS ON LAST PAGE)

		DEWEY NO.	GRID LOCATION
1	MAKING SHARK TOOTH JEWELLERY	700's	7/A
2	DEEP SEA FISHING		
3	BIBLICAL STORY OF THE LOAVES AND FISHES		
4	WHALES		
5	FISH AROUND OUR SHORES		
6	ECOLOGY: IS POLLUTION KILLING FISH		
7	LANGUAGE: A FISHY BUSINESS: GRAMMAR RULES		
8	COMMERCIAL FISHING		
9	INFORMATION ON MICROFICHE		
10	FISHING IN ALASKA AND OTHER ESKIMO COMMUNITIES		
11	FISH 100 DIFFERENT WAYS: RECIPES FOR ALL		

THE BEAUTIFUL MORNING

When I woke up in the morning I pulled the curtains and let the _523_ stream in the window. I patted the _636.7_ on the head and he wagged his tail. I poured some_____in a saucer for the cat. I decided to make some scones for breakfast as a surprise for Mum, so I found a_____book and got cracking. Mum was still asleep. By then it was_____to go to school. I brushed my_____ and _____and got dressed. I rode to school on my_____.

It was a lovely day. Bright_____'s were growing in all the gardens and birds were singing in the_____'s. _____'s were buzzing and_____'s were crawling through the grass. I wished that I owned a_____so that I could ride "clippety clop" through the fields to school. Even better, I wished that I owned a_____so that I could fly to school and swoop high over the mountains like a_____. I wished that I did not have to go to school. I wanted to go_____in the sea like a_____.

Daydreaming of swimming like a fish in the sea I did wheelies into the school gate. There was no one there - no cars, no teachers, no bikes, no pupils. Suddenly I realized why Mum had been asleep. It was Sunday!

(answers on last page)

planets of knowledge

the sea

HOBBIES

ANIMAL KINGDOM

PETS

comets

asteroids

sun

astronomy
DEWEY No:

meteors

moon

telescope

planets

stars

9 and up

Think of all the satellite subjects that are part of the main topic. Use the Subject Index cards to find the Dewey numbers.

inventor's inventory
research activity

USING ENCYCLOPAEDIAS, NON-FICTION BOOKS PERIODICALS etc CHOOSE ANY INVENTION (TELEPHONE, PRINTING PRESS, CHEWING GUM) AND COMPLETE THIS INVENTOR'S INVENTORY.

IF LOTS OF YOUR FRIENDS DO IT YOU CAN STAPLE THE INVENTORIES TOGETHER AND MAKE A BOOK FOR THE LIBRARY, CLASSIFYING IT AT 608 (DEWEY NO. FOR INVENTORS AND INVENTIONS)

NAME OF INVENTION : _____

NAME OF INVENTOR : _____

DATE OF INVENTION : _____

PLACE OF INVENTION : _____

PURPOSE OF INVENTION : _____
_____
_____
_____

HOW IT WORKED : _____
_____
_____
_____
_____
_____
_____
_____
_____
_____
_____

TECHNICAL SPECIFICATIONS : _____
_____
_____
_____
_____

DRAWING OF INVENTION WITH CAPTION
_____
_____
_____

Research Activity * 9 and up

celebrity spot

PERSUADE YOUR FRIENDS TO FILL IN A CELEBRITY SHEET, STAPLE THEM TOGETHER, ADD A TITLE PAGE, COVER. ASK YOUR TEACHER TO MAKE PHOTOCOPIES AND DONATE ONE TO YOUR SCHOOL LIBRARY!

CAPTION _____
_____
_____
_____

NAME : _____

DATE OF BIRTH: _____

PLACE OF BIRTH : _____

PLACE OF RESIDENCE : _____

OCCUPATION : _____

MARRIED / SINGLE / FAMILY : _____

CLAIM TO FAME: _____
_____
_____
_____
_____
_____
_____
_____

MAIN EVENTS IN RISE TO FAME (chronological order) _____
_____
_____
_____

SOURCES OF INFORMATION : _____
_____
_____
_____
_____
_____

CHOOSE SOMEONE FAMOUS — POP STAR, SPORT STAR, ANYONE YOU ADMIRE. FILL IN THIS BIOGRAPHY CHART USING BOOKS, PEOPLE, ENCYCLOPAEDIAS, RECORD JACKETS, MAGAZINES, COMICS — ANY SOURCE OF INFORMATION. STICK IN A PICTURE OR DRAW A PORTRAIT OF THE CELEBRITY. WHEN YOU LIST YOUR SOURCES PUT AUTHOR / TITLE / PAGE IF IT IS A BOOK, NAME OF JOURNAL / VOLUME / DATE / PAGE IF IT IS A MAGAZINE OR PERIODICAL, OR PERSON INTERVIEWED / INTERVIEWER / DATE / PLACE IF A PERSON.

poetry, verse and worse

WHIZZ KID QUIZ

what has <u>doggerel</u> got to do with poetry? (use your dictionary)

_____

A _ _ _ _ _ _ was a minstrel who sang his poetry.

What is the DEWEY NUMBER for <u>poetry</u>? _ _ _ _

Does Dewey count <u>nursery rhymes</u> as poems? Dewey no. _ _ _ _ . _

Are <u>limericks</u> poems in Dewey? Dewey no. _ _ _ _

Are <u>riddles</u> poems in Dewey? Dewey no. _ _ _ _

Would you find <u>funny poems</u> at the same Dewey number as serious poems in your library? Dewey no. _ _ _ _ _

(answers on last page)

Find a poem you really like. Ask your teacher to read it aloud.

POET'S NAME _____

TITLE OF POEM _____

TITLE OF BOOK _____

AUTHOR / EDITOR OF BOOK _____

CLASSIFICATION (DEWEY) NUMBER _____

poetry is fun

FIND A POEM WHICH DESCRIBES CLEARLY WHAT SOMETHING LOOKS LIKE, FEELS LIKE — OR AN EVENT. ASK YOUR TEACHER FOR HELP IF YOU NEED IT. PRACTISE READING YOUR POEM OUT LOUD. ASK YOUR FRIENDS TO DO THE SAME. THEN RECORD YOUR POEMS ON TAPE AND MAKE A **TALKING BOOK** WHICH YOUR TEACHER WILL SEND TO THE **INSTITUTE FOR THE BLIND (FOR THE BLIND** CHILDREN WHO DO NOT HAVE SIGHT AND HAVE TO SEE THEIR WORLD THROUGH WORDS.)

poetry is all about seeing a world through words

---

complete this limerick...

THERE WAS A KEEN POET FROM GORE

WHOSE POEMS WERE AN AWFUL BIG **BORE**

_____

_____

_____

FIND·A·FACT ENCYCLOPAEDIA GAME

10 and up

1   CHOOSE A VOLUME OF THE ENCYCLOPAEDIA BEGINNING WITH
     THE SAME LETTER AS YOUR SURNAME.

2   OPEN IT UP ANYWHERE.   DO NOT READ IT, BUT JUST LET
     YOUR EYE RUN DOWN THE PAGE, SCANNING TO SEE IF ANYTHING
     INTERESTING CATCHES YOUR EYE.

3   WHEN YOU FIND SOMETHING THAT LOOKS INTERESTING, STOP
     AND READ IT CAREFULLY.   IF IT IS NOT REALLY INTERESTING,
     GO ON SCANNING.   IF IT IS INTERESTING, COPY IT OUT
     CAREFULLY BELOW.

Look for the sort of interesting snippet of information that, if
someone said to you "Did you know that....." you would say
"Really? WOW!   You're kidding!"

Make sure you record the SOURCE accurately so that, if someone
does not believe it, they can look it up for themselves.

INTERESTING FACT: ....

....

....

....

....

....

....

Source: Encyclopaedia

Volume number, page

If the whole class does this, you can ask someone to choose the
most interesting facts and make them into a book of facts, like
the "Guinness book of records".

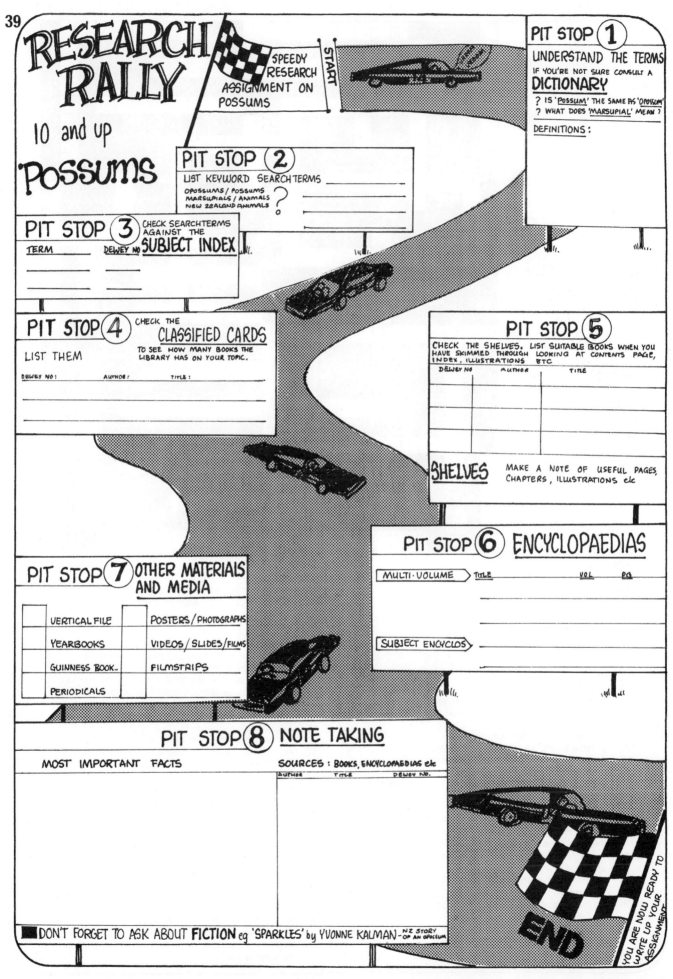

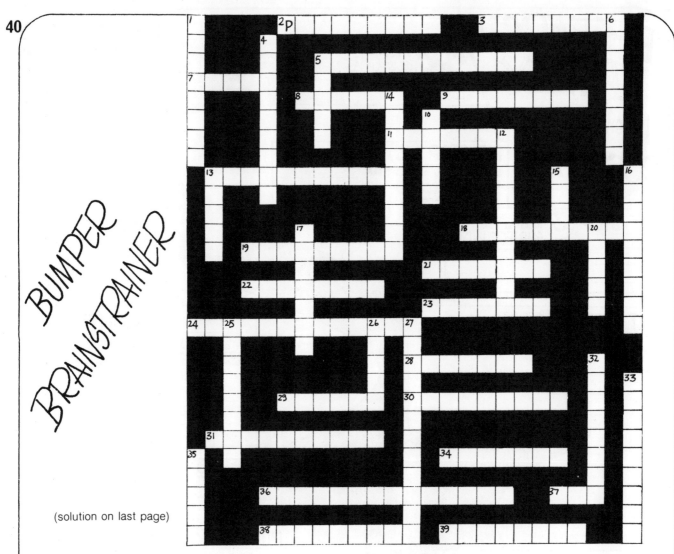

BUMPER BRAINSTRAINER

(solution on last page)

ACROSS

2. Text is divided, each _____ being on a single theme.
3. Words that are opposite in meaning to others.
5. List of suggested reading at the end of a book.
7. The name of a book is its _____.
8. A person who writes books is an _____.
9. Words can be divided into units of sound. One unit is a _____.
11. An invented story.
13. A person who does drawings for a book is an _____
18. A book listing words and their meanings.
19. A cabinet containing records of library holdings on cards.
21. One print run of a book.
22. A table listing what the book contains.
23. An annual publication often containing dates, anniversaries, etc.
24. A book or set of books giving information on all branches of knowledge.
28. An author's introduction to his/her own book.
29. Literary composition in verse is called _____.
30. Each book has a unique identifying number like a car. It is the _____ number. (It is not the Dewey no.)
31. A magazine or publication that is published at regular intervals.
34. A drawing that shows the parts of something or how it works.
36. A system devised to divide knowledge into areas of similarity.
37. A list of words or symbols providing access to a map or diagram.

38. Arrangement of non-fiction on most library shelves is _____.
39. Part of the human body that is also a section at the end of a book with additional information.

DOWN

1. A word that means downwards that is also applied to a file containing loose pamphlet material etc.
4. A dictionary where words of similar meaning are grouped together, the best known being Roget's.
5. Description, usually on front flap of dust-jacket, summarising and praising the book.
6. Words with the same meaning as others.
10. Ratio of measurements on a map or model.
12. Factual information in book form.
13. Alphabetical listing of the detailed contents of a book.
14. Section of books which may only be used in the library.
15. The chief male character in a story.
16. Ownership of the sole legal right to publish or print.
17. Short heading or description under a diagram or illustration.
20. A book of maps.
25. An electronic machine for storing information which is fast replacing traditional card catalogues.
26. The name of the man who invented the most-used system of library classification.
27. The system used for shelf arrangement of fiction in most libraries is _____.
32. List of special or technical words with definitions.
33. An alphabetical listing of names or sources.
35. A drawing consisting of lines showing relationships between quantities.

41

10 and up

WRITING BOOKS

WRITING A BOOK ISN'T LIKE WRITING AN ESSAY OR STORY. IT HELPS TO HAVE A CLEAR IDEA OF THE WHOLE BOOK BEFORE YOU START. TRY SHUTTING YOUR EYES AND VISUALISING IT ALL IN YOUR HEAD. THEN

TO HELP YOU STRUCTURE YOUR BOOK FILL IN THIS **PLANNER**

TYPE OF BOOK YOU WANT TO WRITE : Happy/funny/adventure/ scary/ sad/ exciting /mysterious/ fantasy /science fiction/ everyday life

_____

_____

FOR WHAT AGE LEVEL : your own/ picture book/ illustrated novel with
AND WHAT FORMAT ? chapters/ comic book/ short / long / 1 episode

_____

_____

SETTING ? : Past / Present /future / town / country / imaginary land/ real life /space /school

_____

_____

PLOT ? : What happens to whom, when, how, why? What is the result? How does it affect the people involved? (REMEMBER TO SPACE OUT THE EXCITING PARTS. TOO MUCH EXCITEMENT AND DRAMA CAN BE AS BORING AS TOO MUCH DESCRIPTION)

HOW DOES IT START ? _____

_____

_____

_____

WHAT HAPPENS IN THE MIDDLE ? _____

_____

_____

_____

WHAT HAPPENS IN THE END ? _____

_____

_____

_____

CHARACTERS AND CHARACTERISTICS : old/ young / nice/ nasty /honest /dishonest / kind / mean/ noisy/ quiet / bossy/ rich/ poor/ odd /selfish / jealous / clever/ good at sport / popular / loner

_____

_____

_____

_____

MAKING BOOKS

WRITE YOUR OWN ORIGINAL STORY AND THEN WHEN YOU'RE HAPPY THAT IT'S JUST AS YOU WANT IT, START ON YOUR DUMMY.

DUMMY

CENTRE HEADINGS

LEAVE MARGINS AND PLENTY OF WHITE SPACE AROUND THE TEXT

IF YOU PAINT OR USE FELT TIP PENS FOR THE ILLUSTRATION MAKE SURE YOU USE FAIRLY THICK PAPER.

CHAPTER ONE

Once upon a time there lived a beautiful princess. She lived with her mother and father, the king and queen in a wonderful palace.

MAKE A ROUGH DUMMY OF YOUR BOOK, MAKING SURE THAT YOU LEAVE WIDE MARGINS AND PLAN YOUR TEXT IN BLOCKS. END THE SENTENCES ON THE PAGE. DON'T CARRY HALF SENTENCES OVER.

FINISHED

CHAPTER ONE

Once upon a time there lived a beauti

WHEN YOU ARE SATISFIED WITH THE LANGUAGE, SPELLING AND LAYOUT OF YOUR DUMMY PAGES, PREPARE THE FINISHED PAGES, DRAWING CAREFUL PENCIL LINES FOR TEXT, MARGINS AND CHECKING THE PENCIL SPELLING BEFORE YOU INK IT IN.

ALWAYS DO LETTERING BETWEEN "TRAMLINES" (IN PENCIL). SHORT, FAT LETTERS WITH NOT MUCH SPACE BETWEEN THE LETTERS, BUT QUITE A LOT BETWEEN THE WORDS, LOOK BETTER THAN LONG SPINDLY BADLY SPACED LETTERS

SEW

ONE WAY AND BACK AGAIN THE OTHER WAY, THROUGH THE SAME HOLES AT ABOUT 2½ cm APART

OVER / UNDER / OVER / UNDER / OVER / UNDER / OVER

BOOK CLOTH WRAPPED AROUND THE SPINE

THE HAUNTED CASTLE

BY JAMES BROWN

BROWN & BEAUTIFUL PUBLISHING

IF YOUR BOOK IS THIN, YOU MIGHT WANT TO STAPLE IT. IF IT IS FAT, ASK FOR HELP AND SEW IT.

- CLAMP THE PAGES TOGETHER. CHECK ORDER.
- TAKE A WIDE (5cm) PIECE OF BOOK CLOTH. FOLD IT IN HALF LENGTHWISE AND WRAP IT AROUND THE SPINE OF THE BOOK.
- DRAW A LINE DOWN THE BOOK CLOTH AT ABOUT 1½ cm IN FROM THE SPINE. MAKE MARKS FOR HOLES AT ABOUT 3cm INTERVALS DOWN THIS LINE
- USING A LARGE SAIL NEEDLE AND SAIL THREAD, SEW DOWNWARDS, IN AND OUT, IN ONE DIRECTION AND THEN BACK THROUGH THE SAME HOLES IN THE OTHER DIRECTION.
- KNOT THE FIRST BIT OF THREAD TO THE LAST

P.T.O.

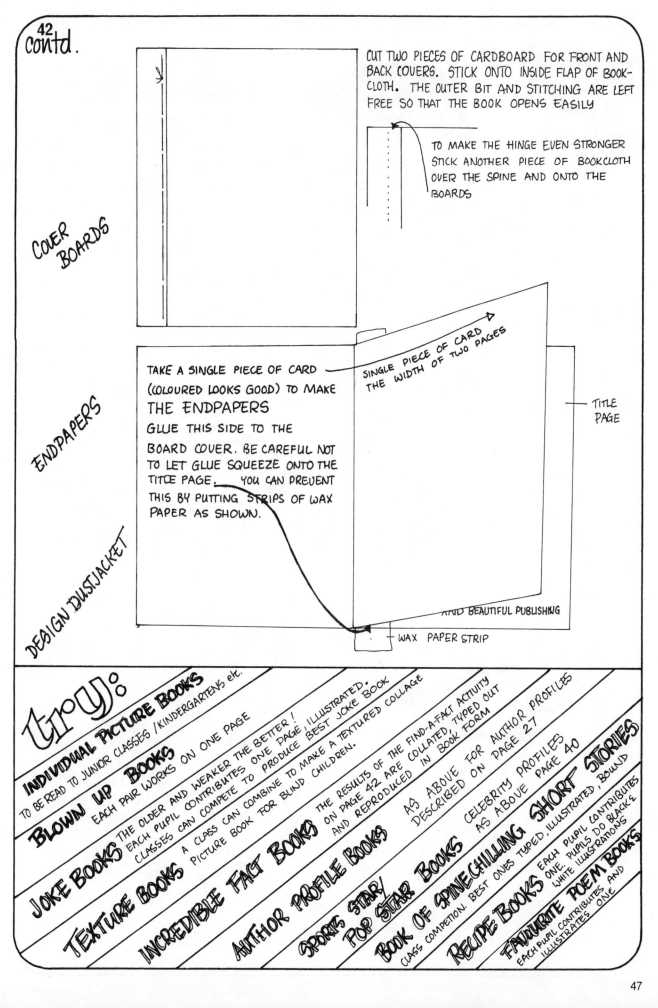

CUT TWO PIECES OF CARDBOARD FOR FRONT AND BACK COVERS. STICK ONTO INSIDE FLAP OF BOOK-CLOTH. THE OUTER BIT AND STITCHING ARE LEFT FREE SO THAT THE BOOK OPENS EASILY

TO MAKE THE HINGE EVEN STRONGER STICK ANOTHER PIECE OF BOOKCLOTH OVER THE SPINE AND ONTO THE BOARDS

COVER BOARDS

ENDPAPERS

DESIGN DUSTJACKET

TAKE A SINGLE PIECE OF CARD (COLOURED LOOKS GOOD) TO MAKE THE ENDPAPERS
GLUE THIS SIDE TO THE BOARD COVER. BE CAREFUL NOT TO LET GLUE SQUEEZE ONTO THE TITLE PAGE.   YOU CAN PREVENT THIS BY PUTTING STRIPS OF WAX PAPER AS SHOWN.

SINGLE PIECE OF CARD THE WIDTH OF TWO PAGES

TITLE PAGE

...AND BEAUTIFUL PUBLISHING

WAX PAPER STRIP

try:

INDIVIDUAL PICTURE BOOKS TO BE READ TO JUNIOR CLASSES / KINDERGARTENS etc.

BLOWN UP BOOKS EACH PAIR WORKS ON ONE PAGE

JOKE BOOKS THE OLDER AND WEAKER THE BETTER! EACH PUPIL CONTRIBUTES ONE PAGE, ILLUSTRATED. CLASSES CAN COMPETE TO PRODUCE BEST JOKE BOOK

TEXTURE BOOKS A CLASS CAN COMBINE TO MAKE A TEXTURED COLLAGE PICTURE BOOK FOR BLIND CHILDREN.

INCREDIBLE FACT BOOKS THE RESULTS OF THE FIND-A-FACT ACTIVITY ON PAGE 42 ARE COLLATED, TYPED OUT AND REPRODUCED IN BOOK FORM

AUTHOR PROFILE BOOKS AS ABOVE FOR AUTHOR PROFILES DESCRIBED ON PAGE 27

SPORTS STAR/ POP STAR BOOKS CELEBRITY PROFILES AS ABOVE PAGE 40

BOOK OF SPINECHILLING SHORT STORIES CLASS COMPETITION. BEST ONES TYPED, ILLUSTRATED, BOUND

RECIPE BOOKS EACH PUPIL CONTRIBUTES ONE. PUPILS DO BLACK & WHITE ILLUSTRATIONS

FAVOURITE POEM BOOKS EACH PUPIL CONTRIBUTES AND ILLUSTRATES ONE

LOADS MORE IDEAS

43
TEACHER'S 3-MIN-DAILY READING SLOT
IN ADDITION TO NORMAL READ-ALOUD PROGRAMME, OF COURSE

Monday	1 Aesop's fable
Tuesday	1 funny poem from Spike Milligan or Michael Rosen
Wednesday	1 newspaper item
Thursday	1 item from Guinness Book of Records
Friday	3 elephant jokes

44
STAFF CHOICE
TEACHERS CHOOSE A FAVOURITE BOOK FROM THE LIBRARY TO DISPLAY UNDER ONE OF THEIR HATS eg

UNDERWATER SWIMMING

VARIATION ON THE BABY PHOTO OR TEDDY BEAR THEME

PUPILS COMPLETE 'GUESS WHO' COMPETITION FORMS

45
PAPERBACK SWAP SHOPS
SWAPPERS BRING BOOKS BEFOREHAND. GET TOKENS (6 FOR GOOD CONDITION, POPULAR TITLE, 1 FOR SHABBY (ₖ) BOOKS PRICED IN ADVANCE (1-5 TOKENS) COMICS AND MAGAZINES TREATED AS BOOKS.

STORYTELLING WORKSHOP
Small groups of children 8-12 work on telling the stories of well-known picture books with suitable dramatic gestures, and perform to junior classes

47
authors illustrators publishers booksellers
SHOW THE FACES BEHIND THE BOOKS
TELL THEM HOW MUCH YOU/YR ... ENJOYED THEIR WORK ... INVITE THEM TO VISIT YOUR SCHOOL ... GIVE THEM V.I.P. TREATMENT ... MAKE SURE THEIR BOOKS HAVE BEEN READ IN ADVANCE ... SEND NEW COPY OF BOOK FOR AUTOGRAPHING

46
CHRISTMAS BOOKLIST
BY VISITING A FRIENDLY LOCAL BOOKSHOP IN SMALL GROUPS, PUPILS CAN COMPILE A "SUGGESTIONS FOR CHRISTMAS PRESENTS" BOOKLIST FOR PARENTS (CONCENTRATING ON PICTURE BOOKS, PAPERBACKS etc) WITH SHORT, DESCRIPTIVE ANNOTATIONS

49
BOOK OF THE MONTH
Taking turns to write short, lively book review BOOK OF THE MONTH for the local newspaper

TEACHER MAKES PRIOR ARRANGEMENT WITH EDITOR

50
MAKING TAPED BOOKS OF ORIGINAL GHOST STORIES BALLADS 'MORAL' TALES TALL TALES LIMERICKS etc
WITH SUITABLE SOUND EFFECTS etc

SUPERBIB

51

PSSSSSST! STILL MORE IDEAS

9 and up

ZIG ZAG CRAZY STORIES

UNFOLD THIS THRILLING TALE ➡

Once upon a time there lived a mouse called MRS FRISBY

Mrs Frisby was invited to DINNER AT ALBERTA'S

There was another guest wearing a black cloak and pointed hat — BADJELLY THE WITCH

"If you don't stop looking at me through those beady little mouse eyes you'll end up like FLAT STANLEY" said BJ

"You're kidding" squeaked MrsF. "I'll call my friend BIG BAD BRUCE who lives with CHARLIE in the CHOCOLATE FACTORY"

"He'll bring DANNY DUNN and ENCYCLOPAEDIA BROWN and..."

"Not while the DARK IS RISING" said BJ menacingly.

"I shall draw my SILVER SWORD and stab your DOGSBODY. There will be THUNDER AND LIGHTNINGS if you don't. stop your squealing said BJ.

"If you stop now we'll go to DINNER AT ALBERTAS and I'll introduce you to THE MAGICIAN'S NEPHEW. If you introduce me to THE OGRE DOWNSTAIRS.

GOOD END OF TERM TREAT. SMALL GROUPS POOL TITLES RECORDED IN THEIR LIBRARY LOGS FOR THE TERM AND PUT THEM TOGETHER TO MAKE A ZIG-ZAG STORY ON FOLDED PAPER. READ ALOUD AND CLASS VOTES FOR THE BEST ONE.

52

USING A 'BUDDY SYSTEM', OLDER READERS HAVE REGULAR TIMES FOR READING TO YOUNGER BUDDY. READING GRANNIES AND GRANDPAS FROM THE COMMUNITY ARE ANOTHER GOOD IDEA.

BOOK BUDDIES

53

FICTION COMIC STRIPS
REDUCING A FICTION BOOK TO COMIC STRIP FORMAT IS A FUN, CHALLENGING OCCASIONAL ACTIVITY

MY SIDE OF THE MOUNTAIN BY JEAN GEORGE

MONTH 1/2 MAY/JUNE
SAM GRIBLEY LEAVES HOME TO FIND THE OLD FAMILY HOME IN THE CATSKILL MOUNTAINS

MONTH 3/4
SAM MAKES HOUSE IN HOLLOW TREE. HE FISHES AND LEARNS TO TRAP. HE BEFRIENDS ANIMALS

MONTH 5/6

MONTH 7/8

MONTH 9/10

MONTH 11

MONTH 12

MONTH 13

END

54

taped group tales

PUPILS WORK IN SMALL GROUPS WITH TAPE RECORDER. EACH GROUP IS GIVEN THE TITLE OF A STORY, EG 'THE NIGHT THE DOOR CREAKED OPEN'. THEY HAVE APPROX. ½ HOUR TO WORK TOGETHER TO MAKE UP THE BEGINNING OF THE STORY. ONE PUPIL TRANSCRIBES IT. IT IS TYPED AND REPRODUCED. EACH MEMBER OF THE GROUP THEN HAS TO MAKE UP AN INDIVIDUAL ENDING FOR THE STORY. SUCCESSFUL ATTEMPTS CAN BE MADE INTO BOOKS FOR THE SCHOOL LIBRARY.

skills index

The term 'library skills' covers a wide range of reading, research and information retrieval skills. Many of these are interdependent and cannot be taught independently in out-of-context lock-step drill fashion.

As important as any skill is the pupil's attitude to it. Many of these activities are designed to build confidence, familiarity, and enthusiasm in the use of the library's stock and systems.

Four main skills are highlighted:

1 Locational

Finding way round the library, its materials and systems.

2 Alphabetical

Applied to Subject Index, indexes, filing rules, dictionaries, encyclopaedias, arrangement of fiction sequence on shelves.

3 Numerical

Dewey system applied to filing of classified (Dewey) cards and arrangement of non-fiction books (and non-book media) on the shelves.

4 Research

• Retrieval: Applying locational, alphabetic, numeric skills to the retrieval of material, using catalogue and indexes as tool, defining search with main headings and subfields.

• Bibliographical: Recording sources (author, title, publisher, date etc.) so that information can be checked or relocated.

• Reading for research: Being able to read purposefully (looking for answers to specific questions), skim reading, scanning, reading in depth, comparative, analytical, evaluative reading, being able to assess style (factual/personal/anecdotal/inferential) for bias, viewpoint, intention.

• Notetaking and beyond: Being able to comprehend, summarise, interpret, concisely and creatively.

aim / scope	activity no.	attitude	skill
who - the user To familiarize the teacher with the pupils' reading needs and habits. To encourage pupils to explore the school library and its resources and to regard it as *their* library To encourage pupils to regard themselves as library users & readers	**1** READER PROFILE	POSITIVE ATTITUDE TOWARDS LIBRARY USE AND READING.	— COMPREHENSION — QUESTIONNAIRE SKILLS — EVALUATION SKILLS — STORYING
	2 I'M A READER	ENTHUSIASM FOR BOOKS AND LIBRARY USE. IDENTITY AS A READER.	— LOCATING & RECORDING AUTHOR & TITLE — EVALUATION
	3 BROWSING PADDLE	CONFIDENCE IN BROWSING AND SELECTING BOOKS FOR YOUNG READERS.	— BROWSING /RETRIEVAL SKILLS — CONFIDENT, INDEPENDENT BOOK SELECTION.
	4 MINI·QUIZ 7-9's	CONFIDENCE IN HANDLING LIBRARY / BOOK LANGUAGE.	— FAMILIARITY WITH LIBRARY/ BOOK TERMINOLOGY
	5 YOGHURT POT READING RECORDS	SATISFACTION IN GAINING IDENTITY AS A 'REAL' READER, & IN BUILDING UP A RECORD OF READING MILEAGE AND OPINIONS.	— BIBLIOGRAPHIC SKILLS (RECORDING AUTHOR / TITLE) — EVALUATIVE SKILLS (RECORDING OPINION) — RECALL
	6 LIBRARY FOLDER	SATISFACTION IN HAVING A PLACE TO PUT ALL YOUR LIBRARY WORK AND SEEING IT BUILD UP. GIVING THE LIBRARY STATUS AS A VITAL AREA OF LEARNING AND ENCOURAGING INVOLVEMENT.	
what - the library To explain :- ● Purpose of library:— books to enjoy— stories, information ● Borrowing procedures ● Opening hours and library rules ● Role of the library staff ● Book care & appreciation ● How to use the systems to find materials ● How to use materials to find information. To encourage pupils to become familiar, confident users of the library, knowing what is expected of them as users and knowing what benefits they can expect from the library's stock, systems and staff in terms of reading enjoyment and information	**7** LIBRARY LOG	FEELING OF IDENTITY AND VALUE AS A READER. HAVING A CONTEXT FOR READING. 'PERSONALIZING' AND HAVING PRACTICAL CONTEXT FOR LEARNING 'PARTS OF A BOOK'.	— BIBLIOGRAPHIC SKILLS (RECORDING AUTHOR & TITLE) — FUNCTION OF DIFFERENT PARTS OF A BOOK — EVALUATIVE SKILLS (OPINIONS & RATINGS)
	8 LIBRARY MAP	CONFIDENCE WITH LIBRARY TERMS LIKE 'VERTICAL FILE', IDENTIFYING, LOCATING AND UNDERSTANDING THEIR FUNCTION.	— LOCATIONAL SKILLS — MAPPING SKILLS — LIBRARY FAMILIARITY
	9 BOOK CARE BOOK MARKS & POSTERS	POSITIVE ATTITUDE TOWARDS CARE AND HANDLING OF BOOKS.	— BOOK HANDLING AND CARE SKILLS
	10 BOOK POSTERS	POSITIVE ATTITUDE TOWARDS BOOKS AND LIBRARIES. SEEING BOOKS AND LIBRARIES AS A SOURCE OF INTERESTING ACTIVITIES AND FUN RATHER THAN JUST AS THE STORAGE PLACE FOR SCHOOL / COMMUNITY READING AND LEARNING RESOURCES.	— LANGUAGE SKILLS (LANGUAGE OF PROMOTION AND ADVERTISING) — DISPLAY SKILLS (art/design)
	11 DESIGN A SPACE-AGE LIBRARY	ENTHUSIASM FOR THE LIBRARY AS A PLACE WHERE THINGS HAPPEN. SEEING LIBRARIES AS AN EVOLVING SOCIAL CONCEPT AND FUNCTION RATHER THAN AS A STATIC PLACE OF STORAGE. ANALYSING AND COMPARING THE FUNCTIONS OF DIFFERENT LIBRARIES – PUBLIC / SCHOOL etc. FOCUSING ON MEDIA OTHER THAN BOOKS, ON TECHNOLOGY, COMPUTERS IN LIBRARIES etc.	— PROVIDING CONTEXT FOR RECALL AND APPLICATION OF SKILLS ACQUIRED TO DATE — EVALUATION OF ROLE OF LIBRARY IN SOCIETY — EVALUATION OF TECHNOLOGY IN RELATION TO LIBRARIES AND INFORMATION

aim / scope	activity no.	attitude	skill
what - materials ● FICTION ● NON·FICTION ● REFERENCE BOOKS ● VERTICAL FILE (PAMPHLETS etc) ● PERIODICALS ● NON·BOOK MEDIA (POSTERS, FILMS, FILMSTRIPS, SLIDES, VIDEOS, KITS etc) AIM: To introduce pupils to [and to promote] the wide range of fiction and non fiction in the library : how it is stored ; how it can be retrieved ; how it can be evaluated, enjoyed, remembered, recorded Ensuring that pupils understand the principle of shelving fiction alphabetically by author's surname Encouraging pupils to keep a record of their reading and to share their opinions of books and authors.	**12** AUTHORS' TOP TEN	FAMILIARITY WITH CONCEPT OF AUTHORSHIP AS KEY FACTOR IN ORGANIZATION OF FICTION ON SHELVES.	— REINFORCEMENT OF CONCEPT OF AUTHORSHIP IN FICTION — ACQUAINTANCE WITH WIDE RANGE OF AUTHORS & TITLES — EVALUATIVE / BIBLIOGRAPHIC
	13 FICTION DETECTIVE GAME	FAMILIARITY WITH AND CONFIDENCE IN USING FICTION CATALOGUE, RELATING THE ORGANIZATION OF THE FICTION CATALOGUE TO THE FICTION SHELVES.	— RELATING ALPHABETICAL SKILLS TO CATALOGUE RETRIEVAL SKILLS. — FINDING AUTHOR'S NAME BY LOOKING UP TITLE CARDS. — FINDING TITLES BY AN AUTHOR STOCKED BY THE LIBRARY BY LOOKING UP AUTHOR CARDS
	14 ALPHABETIC SURNAMES	FAMILIARITY WITH CONCEPT OF AUTHOR'S SURNAME AS FILING WORD, ISOLATING THE FIRST THREE LETTERS. CONFIDENCE IN APPLYING ALPHABETIC SKILLS TO THE RETRIEVAL OF FICTION BY AUTHOR.	— ALPHABETICAL SKILLS — LOCATIONAL SKILLS [RELATING SURNAME TO SHELF ARRANGEMENT OF FICTION]
	15 FICTION FILING GAME	CONTRIBUTING SENSE OF LANGUAGE AS FUN, ELASTIC. FUN PRACTICE OF CONCEPT OF ALPHABETICAL ORGANIZATION BY AUTHOR'S SURNAME.	— ALPHABETICAL SKILLS — LANGUAGE SKILLS (Fun for those who can & helps diagnose those who haven't yet understood) — DISPLAY AND PRESENTATION SKILLS
	16 THE CASE OF THE BORING BOOK	EXCITES PERVERSE ENTHUSIASM AND A LOT OF POSITIVE DEBATE ON "ONE PERSON'S MEAT..." ENCOURAGES ANALYSIS OF FREQUENT 'DEAD BORING' JUDGMENT PASSED ON BOOKS. GOOD FORUM FOR DISCUSSION ON CRITERIA FOR GOOD BOOKS etc.	— EVALUATION — DISCRIMINATION — CRITICAL & OBJECTIVE ASSESSMENT — LANGUAGE SKILLS [formal / judicial language]
	17 FICTION CARDS	HAVING A CONTEXT FOR READING. CONTRIBUTING TO A WAY OF SHARING GOOD READING. SATISFACTION IN READING WHAT PEERS HAVE RATED HIGHLY.	— CRITICAL & EVALUATIVE SKILLS — BIBLIOGRAPHIC SKILLS
	18 FICTION AUCTION	AS ABOVE	— CRITICAL & EVALUATIVE SKILLS — LANGUAGE SKILLS [LANGUAGE OF PROMOTION AND SELLING]

aim / scope	activity no.	attitude	skill
▶ what: fiction contd.	**19** SPACE AGE READING RECORDS	HAVING A CONTEXT FOR READING & REMEMBERING BOOKS AND AUTHORS PROVIDES A SPUR TO WANT TO READ MORE.	— EVALUATIVE SKILLS [★ RATING] — BIBLIOGRAPHIC SKILLS [RECORDING AUTHOR, TITLE]
	20 SURFSAILER READING RECORDS	AS ABOVE	AS ABOVE
	21 READING RECORD BALLOONS	AS ABOVE	AS ABOVE
	22 CLASS READING RECORDS	AS ABOVE BUT WITH EMPHASIS ON GROUP PARTICIPATION AND ENJOYING SEEING A CLASS EFFORT GROW.	AS ABOVE
	23 BOOK REVIEW SKELETON	SATISFACTION IN ANALYSING THE MAIN PLOT / THEME / CHARACTERS OF A STORY AND MAKING AN EFFECTIVE MOBILE OR FRIEZE.	— ANALYTICAL SKILLS — EVALUATIVE SKILLS — BIBLIOGRAPHIC SKILLS — WRITING SKILLS [SUMMARY / SYNOPSIS]
	24 BOOK REVIEWS THE FUN WAY	AS ABOVE	AS ABOVE PLUS — LANGUAGE SKILLS [LANGUAGE OF SELLING, ADVERTISING]
	25 AUTHOR PROFILE	BECOMING FAMILIAR WITH AUTHORS AS 'REAL LIVE PEOPLE', PROVIDING SPUR TO WRITE TO AUTHORS etc.	— RESEARCH SKILLS — NOTE-TAKING SKILLS
	26 GOODIES & BADDIES IN FICTION	ENCOURAGING AND PROVIDING CONTEXT FOR ANALYSING THE BEHAVIOUR, MOTIVES AND PERSONALITIES OF FICTIONAL CHARACTERS.	— BIBLIOGRAPHIC — RECALL — CHARACTER ANALYSIS AND EVALUATION, [GIVING REASONS FOR OPINION]

aim / scope	activity no.	attitude	skill
what - non fiction **DEWEY** To encourage pupils to become familiar with the skill of retrieving material classified numerically by the Dewey Decimal System, so that they can apply it in their classroom-based research assignments.	**27** HITCH-HIKERS' GUIDE TO THE CARD CATALOGUE	EASE AND CONFIDENCE IN USING THE CATALOGUE AS A RESEARCH TOOL.	— BEING ABLE TO IDENTIFY WHICH PART OF THE CATALOGUE TO SEARCH FOR SPECIFIC RESEARCH NEEDS
	28 DEWEY STORY	SEEING DEWEY AS A SYSTEM BASED ON LOGIC WITH EACH DIGIT MEANING SOMETHING — NOT JUST A RANDOM COLLECTION OF NUMBERS.	— ABILITY TO COMPREHEND AND MANIPULATE A SYSTEM OF ORGANISING KNOWLEDGE INTO TEN CLASSES OR CATEGORIES, AND GROUPING LIKE MATERIAL TOGETHER WITHIN EACH CLASS
	29 DEWEY MOBILE	UNDERSTANDING DEWEY BECOMES EASIER WITH PRACTICAL EXERCISES INVOLVING THE USE OF THE <u>SUBJECT INDEX</u> CARDS.	— ABILITY TO LOOK UP A <u>SUBJECT</u> IN THE <u>SUBJECT INDEX</u> TO FIND THE <u>DEWEY NUMBER</u> RELATING TO THAT SUBJECT — THE FIRST STEP IN ALL LIBRARY-BASED RESEARCH
	30 KEYWORD SEARCHTERMS	RESEARCH BECOMES MUCH EASIER IF FIRST STEPS ARE TAKEN SLOWLY AND SYSTEMATICALLY. DEFINING SEARCHTERMS CAN BE DAUNTING AND PRACTICE IS NEEDED.	— BEING ABLE TO THINK FROM <u>GENERAL</u> TOPIC TO <u>PARTICULAR SUBFIELD/s</u> OR <u>PARTICULAR</u> ASPECT BACK TO <u>GENERAL</u> TOPIC. — CATEGORIZING AND CLASSIFICATION SKILLS — LOGICAL THINKING SKILLS
	31 DEWEY MOBILE MARK <u>II</u>	UNDERSTANDING THE LOGIC OF DEWEY CLASSES AND SUBFIELDS [eg SPORT 796 FOOTBALL 796·33] THE FUN WAY	— DEWEY SKILLS RELATED TO SUBJECT INDEX USE FOR RETRIEVING DEWEY NUMBER
	32 DEWEY LOCATER	FINDING ARRANGEMENT OF NON-FICTION SECTION OF THE LIBRARY BY DEWEY INTERESTING AND CHALLENGING RATHER THAN DAUNTING.	— MAPPING SKILLS — APPLICATION OF THE THEORY OF DEWEY TO THE ARRANGEMENT OF NON-FICTION ON THE SHELVES
	33 BEAUTIFUL MORNING - DEWEY CLOZE GAME	USING SUBJECT INDEX AND CLASSIFIED CARDS TO EXTEND FAMILIARITY WITH THE CONCEPT OF NUMBERS REPRESENTING SUBJECTS - A FUN APPROACH OPEN TO MANY VARIATIONS.	— ALPHABETIC SKILLS — NUMERIC SKILLS
	34 PLANETS OF KNOWLEDGE	SEEING HOW DEWEY SYSTEM, KEYWORDS AND SUBFIELDS INTERRELATE IS EASY AND FUN WHEN IT IS PRESENTED GRAPHICALLY.	— RELATING AND RECAPITULATING SKILLS ACHIEVED SO FAR [DEWEY/KEYWORD/ SUBJECT INDEX SKILLS]

aim/scope	activity no.	attitude	skill
RESEARCH Encouraging pupils to explore the spread of Dewey, and a wide range of books and other materials so that the information they retrieve is relevant to their curriculum needs **but** also relevant to their own personal interests and information needs. Research materials should include phone directories, time-tables, catalogues, newspapers, TV programmes etc	**35** INVENTOR'S INVENTORY	INTEREST AND ENTHUSIASM ARE AROUSED WITH A SHORT RESEARCH TASK ASKING SPECIFIC QUESTIONS WHICH DEMONSTRATE THE PRACTICAL USE OF THE SKILLS AND TECHNIQUES LEARNT SO FAR.	— RESEARCH USING VARIETY OF SOURCES [NON-FICTION, ENCYCLOPAEDIAS etc]
	36 CELEBRITY SPOT	AS ABOVE	AS ABOVE
	37 POETRY, VERSE AND WORSE	ENJOYMENT OF PLASTICITY, FUN AND CHALLENGE OF LANGUAGE.	— CRITICAL SKILLS — LISTENING SKILLS — CREATIVE LANGUAGE SKILLS — DEWEY THROUGH SUBJECT INDEX SKILLS
	38 FIND-A-FACT GAME	THE POPULARITY OF THE 'GUINNESS BOOK OF RECORDS' SETS THE PRECEDENT FOR THE ENTHUSIASM THIS ENCYCLOPAEDIA RESEARCH ENGENDERS.	— ENCYCLOPAEDIA RESEARCH SKILLS – ALPHABETIC — USING INDEX — READING SKILLS : — SCANNING — SKIMMING — PURPOSIVE
	39 RESEARCH RALLY	INTEREST IN SEEING HOW INDIVIDUAL SKILLS AND SOURCES INTERWEAVE AS PART OF THE RESEARCH PROCESS.	— SYSTEMATIC INFORMATION RETRIEVAL PATTERN AND PROCEDURE. [ABSOLUTELY VITAL TO RECAP ON PREVIOUS LEARNING]
	40 BUMPER BRAINSTRAINER	CHALLENGE TO SHOW OFF KNOWLEDGE OR REFRESH JADED MEMORIES.	— RECAP ON LIBRARY/ BOOK TERMINOLOGY
AUTHORSHIP 'Teaching' 'parts of a book' can kill the pupil's interest in books and reading. There's no better way to learn about books than writing your own.	**41** WRITING BOOKS	HAVING A FRAMEWORK ENCOURAGES THE TENTATIVE AUTHOR TO BEGIN.	— LANGUAGE, NARRATIVE SKILLS OF SELF EXPRESSION WITHIN STRUCTURE OF BOOK [PICTURE BOOK/ NOVEL/ BIOGRAPHY /DIARY etc]
	42 MAKING BOOKS	BY BEING ENCOURAGED TO WRITE A <u>BOOK</u> FROM THE START YOU SEE YOURSELF AS A 'REAL' AUTHOR, VISUALIZING YOUR BOOK AS A FINISHED <u>PRODUCT</u>. [DIFFERENT EMPHASIS FROM WRITING & STAPLING IT INTO BOOK FORM LATER]	— WRITING SKILLS [PURPOSIVE WRITING - WRITING AS AUTHOR WITH INTENTION OF PRODUCING A BOOK] — EDITING SKILLS — PRESENTATION SKILLS — 'PARTS OF A BOOK' IN CONTEXT
Bearing in mind that all these ideas should be part of a structured planned library programme, not one-off lesson fillers	**43-54** LOADS MORE IDEAS	VARIED IDEAS FOR MAKING LIBRARY LESSONS INTO LIVELY LESSONS AND ENCOURAGING FAMILIARITY AND ENTHUSIASM WITH BOOKS, AUTHORS AND LIBRARY ACTIVITIES. GIVING PUPILS THE OPPORTUNITY TO PROVIDE PROOF OF THE PUDDING— THAT THE 'LIBRARY SKILLS' PUPILS REMEMBER ARE THOSE TAUGHT IN A PRACTICAL AND ENJOYABLE CONTEXT.	COMBINING, REINFORCING AND GIVING PRACTICE IN VARIOUS SKILLS AND ATTITUDES DEVELOPED IN ACTIVITIES 1—40 WITH AN EMPHASIS ON <u>LISTENING</u> ACTIVITIES WHICH SHOULD BE PART OF THE SCHOOL DAY OF ALL PUPILS OF ALL AGES

programme planner

NB! TO COMPLEMENT AND SUPPLEMENT CLASSROOM-BASED READING & RESEARCH - NOT A STAND-ALONE SCHEME

AGE	TERM 1 library	reading	research	TERM 2 library	reading	research	TERM 3 library	reading	research	EMPHASIS
5-6	ORAL INTRODUCTION TO WHICH BOOKS CAN BE BORROWED, HOW WHERE AND WHEN.	2 I'M A READER		3 BROWSING PADDLE 2 cont'd	22 BOOK WORM READING RECORDS		3 cont'd.	2 cont'd 22 cont'd	INFORMAL INTRODUCTION TO SIMPLE FACT BOOKS	Emphasis on teacher reading wide & varied selection of marvellous books throughout the year.
7	3 BROWSING PADDLE 4 MINI QUIZ ORAL RECAP.	YOGHURT POT 5 READING RECORDS		9 BOOK CARE BOOK MARKS	22 READING KITES 5 cont'd		22 KITES cont'd 5 cont'd	4 MINI QUIZ 7-9's		Emphasis on making child comfortable as a reader in the library.
8	ORAL RECAP 4 MINI QUIZ 7-9's	10 BOOK POSTERS			22 READING TREES		42 COMPILE JOKE BOOK	30 KEYWORDS		As above, encouraging reading and also introducing concept of searching for non-fiction by SUBJECT
9	8 LIBRARY MAP ORAL RECAP	17 FICTION CARDS	29 KEYWORDS		24 TRIANGULAR REVIEW 21 BALLOON READING RECORDS	30 KEYWORDS (more sophisticated)	42 COMPILE RECIPE BOOK	28 DEWEY STORY	29 DEWEY MOBILE	Ensuring that alphabetical and numerical filing skills have been taught. Emphasis on SUBJECT INDEX
10	8 LIBRARY MAP ORAL RECAP	17 FICTION CARDS 14 ALPHABETICAL SURNAMES	28 DEWEY STORY 32 DEWEY LOCATER	9 BOOK CARE BOOK MARKS	13 FICTION DETECTIVE 20 SURFSAILER READING RECORDS	27 HITCHHIKERS' GUIDE	10 BOOK POSTERS	12 AUTHOR'S TOP 10 37 POETRY, VERSE	33 DEWEY CLOZE	Ensuring that alph. & numerical skills can be applied to retrieval of fiction and non-fiction from shelves. Emphasis on SUBJECT INDEX.
11	6 LIBRARY FOLDER 1 READER PROFILE ORAL RECAP	7 LOG 17 FICTION CARDS 14 ALPHABETICAL SURNAMES	25 AUTHOR PROFILE	6 cont'd	15 FICTION FILING 17 cont'd 19 SPACE AGE READING RECORDS 7 cont'd	27 HITCHHIKERS GUIDE	6 cont'd	7 cont'd 17 cont'd 26 GOODIES & BADDIES 46 XMAS BOOKLIST	31 DEWEY MOBILE II	Reinforcing SUBJECT INDEX skills. Emphasis on opinion in reading. Practice in application of DEWEY skills
12	6 LIBRARY FOLDER 1 READER PROFILE ORAL RECAP	7 LOG 17 FICTION CARDS	34 PLANETS OF KNOWL. 33 DEWEY CLOZE	6 cont'd	4/2 PICTURE BOOKS 17 cont'd 7 cont'd 23 REVIEW SKELETON	35 INVENTORS INVENTORY	6 cont'd	7 cont'd 17 cont'd 16 CASE OF BORING BOOK	38 FINDAFACT 36 CELEBRITY SPOT	As above but through writing / binding books, emphasis on books, authorship book language / publishing etc
13	6 LIBRARY FOLDER 1 READER PROFILE ORAL RECAP	7 LOG 17 FICTION CARDS 52 BUDDY READERS	40 BRAINSTRAINER 36 CELEBRITY SPOT	6 cont'd	53 COMIC STRIPS 17 cont'd 7 cont'd 52 cont'd	SPACE-AGE LIBRARY	6 cont'd	7 cont'd 17 cont'd 18 FICTION AUCTION	39 RESEARCH RALLY	Complement to classroom research & diagnostic function - showing pupils who still can't cope.

answers

Activity 4

Authors/libraries/fantastic/…/fiction/non-fiction/encyclopaedias/dictionaries/
reference books/catalogue/author/title/reading logs

Activity 5

8	11	12	7	6	14	9	1	5	2
ADD /	ALP /	APP /	BEA /	BEN /	DAR /	LEG /	NAP /	ODI /	PAG /

3	13	10	4
POP /	RES /	TOO /	WOL

Activity 27

1 Look up the SUBJECT INDEX CARDS
2 Look up the FICTION TITLE CARDS
3 Look up the CLASSIFIED (DEWEY) CARDS
4 Look up the FICTION AUTHOR CARDS

Activity 29

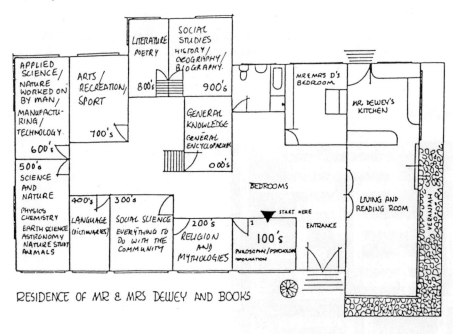

RESIDENCE OF MR & MRS DEWEY AND BOOKS

Activity 30

SPORT 796   PETS 636.6   CRAFTWORK 745.5

Activity 32

1	700's	7/A		6	300's	1/C
2	700's	8/A		7	400's	1/A
3	200's	1/D		8	600's	6/A
4	500's	5/A		9	100's	1/E
5	500's	5/A		10	900's	8/E
				11	600's	5/A

Activity 33

523 or 523.7 (sun), 636.7 (dog), 637 (milk), 641.5 (recipe), 529 (time), 612 (teeth), 612 (hair), 388 or 388.2 or 629.2 (bike), 583 or 635 (flowers/gardening), 582.16 (trees), 595.7 (bees), 595.7 (insects), 798 or 636.1 (horse), 598 (bird), 797.2 (swimming), 597 (fish)

Activity 37

Doggerel is bad verse/ Bard/ 821 (English poetry)/ Nursery rhymes = 398.8/ Limericks = 827/ Riddles = 793.7/ Humorous verse = 827

Activity 40

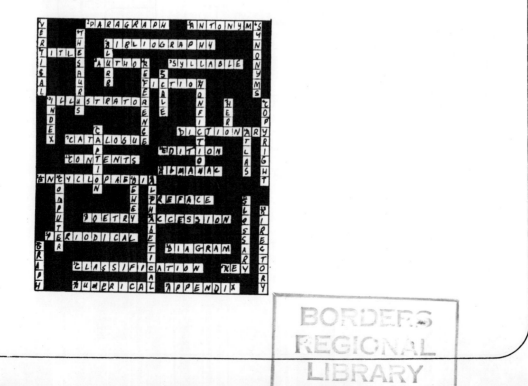

The Dewey Decimal Classification for School Libraries 4th Ed. Compiled by Mary L. South, Forest Press/SLA, 1986. Distributed in Britain by Don Gresswell Ltd. Further simplifications are often made. Rely on the numbers already in use (as shown by the subject index) in your library.